Dear Friend,

Every book is an adventure waiting to be shared.
With each page, a story unfolds, providing the reader
a glimpse into new worlds and ideas. Books are a
magic tool, sparking the imagination, and fueling a
passion for knowledge and exploration. My family
and I hope this book inspires you to continue seeking
new adventures.

Joel Quadracci and Family
Avid readers, dreamers & explorers

TIME
FOR KIDS

BIG
BOOK OF
WHY

© 2016 Time Inc. Books

Published by Liberty Street, an imprint of Time Inc. Books
225 Liberty Street
New York, New York 10281

Special thanks to the Time Inc. Books team: Margot Schupf, Anja Schmidt, Beth Sutinis, Deirdre Langeland, Georgia Morrissey, Alex Voznesenskiy and Hillary Leary, and to Andrea Delbanco and Nellie Cutler at *Time for Kids*

Created at Oomf, Inc.
www.Oomf.com

By: Mark Shulman and K.C. Kelley
Designed by: Oomf, Inc.
Researchers: Amy Lennard Goehner, Dr. Philip Nash
Educational Consultant: Kara Pranikoff
Proofreading: Nancy Vergara
Indexer: Wendy Allex
Contributors: John Perritano, Deirdre Langeland
Special Thanks: Jim Cheng, Erica Davis, Patty Kelley, Bill Madrid, Leah Ragen, Miriam Ragen, Susan Rolander, Seymour Simon

ISBN 10: 1-61893-164-4
ISBN 13: 978-1-61893-164-1
Library of Congress Control Number: 2016930817

Second Edition, 2016

1 QGT 16

10 9 8 7 6 5 4 3 2 1

Time Inc. Books products may be purchased for business or promotional use. For information on bulk purchases, please contact Christi Crowley in the Special Sales Department at (845) 895-9858.

We welcome your comments and suggestions about Time Inc. Books.

Please write to us at:
Time Inc. Books
Attention: Book Editors
P.O. Box 62310
Tampa, Florida 33662-2310

timeincbooks.com

CONTENTS

Why do some sheep get painted?

Page 19

Why are dogs' noses wet?

While the noses of many dogs are wet, plenty of dogs have dry ones. What keeps a dog's snout moist? No one knows for sure. One theory says that the wetness comes from mucus produced inside Fido's nose. Another hypothesis suggests that because dogs lick their noses all the time, saliva keeps their noses moist. Despite popular belief, a warm nose does not mean a dog is sick.

Why do dogs turn around before lying down?

Dogs will often circle the bed or carpet two or three times before curling up and going to sleep. Are they checking for bed bugs or snakes? Not necessarily. Many times dogs are just flattening out their beds to get comfortable. Actually, this behavior is most likely a genetic trait left over from when the dog's ancestors used to dig their own shelters. After digging, the dogs would feel comfortable in their dens and plop down for some much needed shut-eye.

WHY DO WOLVES AND DOGS LOOK SO MUCH ALIKE?

Scientists say that dogs evolved from wolves thousands of years ago. Scientists who compared dog and wolf DNA believe that every dog—from Chihuahuas to Great Danes—is descended from wolves. Those long-ago forest hunters are the mothers of all modern dogs.

Why are chimpanzees disappearing?

Chimpanzees—who are closely related to humans— are a well-known great ape. Their native habitat is the rainforests of central Africa. That habitat has been shrinking for decades as people cut down trees, build farms, and cause pollution that harms the forest. A population of millions of chimps has shrunk to less than 300,000.

Why are apes so much like humans?

We might look different from gorillas, but humans and apes have many things in common. We share about 99% of our genes with apes, and apes—chiefly chimpanzees—create cultures just like humans. A culture is a learned way of living passed down from one generation to the next. Most researchers agree that humans and chimps diverged from a common ancestor about 5 to 7 million years ago.

An adult gorilla can weigh up to 452 pounds (205 kg).

WHAT MAKES APES AND MONKEYS DIFFERENT?

Although apes and monkeys all belong to a group of animals called primates, they are different from one another. Apes are very large and live mostly on or near the ground. They don't have tails. Monkeys have tails, and some species have prehensile tails, which means they can be used to grasp things like branches. Apes are also bigger than monkeys and have broad backs. Apes seem to be smarter than monkeys, too. They can learn sign language and use tools, such as sticks and rocks.

Why do vampire bats drink blood?

There are many different types of bats, but there's only one type that drinks blood—the vampire bat. In fact, they are the only mammals that feed entirely on blood. Scientists say the first vampire bats were related to bats that gorged themselves on the parasites of prehistoric beasts. Vampire bats mainly drink the blood of cows, horses, pigs, and birds.

Why do bats hang upside-down?

The main reason bats stay up high is to avoid predators. Bats evolved special feet and joints that make it easy for them to hang that way for a long time, even while sleeping. Hanging from high tree branches or cave ceilings makes the bats difficult to reach, so being upside down means staying alive!

WHY DO BATS USE ECHOLOCATION?

Animals that use echolocation make a sound, and then use its echo to locate objects like walls and ceilings. Bats use echolocation to keep from flying into buildings and trees, emitting a high-frequency sound that humans cannot hear. Bats also use echolocation to detect their favorite meal—bugs—and to avoid predators.

Why can't fish breathe when **out of water?**

Fish need oxygen to live, just like humans. But while humans use their lungs to take in oxygen from the air, fish are designed to take oxygen from water. The water passes through a fish's mouth and over a set of gills, which absorb oxygen. Without lungs, a fish out of water is a fish without oxygen.

Gills absorb oxygen from the water.

WHY DO MOST FISH HAVE SCALES?

Scales act as a kind of armor, helping protect the skin of fish. Scales also help water move more smoothly over a fish as it swims. Even so, some fish, such as catfish and lampreys, have no scales.

Why are crocodiles and alligators different?

Crocodiles and alligators are distant cousins with some differences. Alligators have wide U-shaped snouts, while the snouts of crocodiles are V-shaped. Some crocodiles prefer to live in saltwater habitats, while alligators most often have freshwater homes. You can find alligators only in the United States and China. Crocodiles live in Mexico, Central America, South America, Africa, Southeast Asia, and Australia.

WHY ARE CROCODILES GOOD SWIMMERS?

The tail of a crocodile is huge and strong. In the water, crocodiles use their tails for power. Crocodiles swim by pressing their legs flat against their bodies. Using one webbed foot as a rudder, they propel themselves forward, moving their strong tails back and forth. Crocodiles can swim up to 6 miles (10 km) per hour.

Female crocodiles can lay 25 to 80 eggs at one time!

Alligators have been around for 150 million years.

Why do some bugs glow in the dark?

Who doesn't love glow-in-the-dark Halloween costumes, stickers, or glow sticks? Many bugs glow in the dark, too. Unlike glow toys, these bugs make their own light. These bugs are bioluminescent (by-oh-lew-muh-NESS-ent). Chemicals in their bodies combine to make them shine. Although bioluminescent animals light up, they don't give off heat like a light bulb does. Fireflies are the most common glow-in-the-dark insects. They light up to communicate with each other as they look for a mate.

WHY DO SOME SCORPIONS GLOW?

In ultraviolet light, some types of scorpions glow blue. Their exoskeletons are reacting to a type of light that human eyes can't see. Scientists are not sure just why this happens to scorpions. One theory is that the glow warns them when parts of their body aren't properly hidden, and could give them away.

WHY DO SOME FISH GIVE OFF THEIR OWN LIGHT?

Glowing fish use their light for different reasons. Deep in the ocean, some bioluminescent fish turn on the lights to attract their next meal. Other animals use light to blind predators that try to stalk and eat them. Some species create light to blend in with their surroundings. Some worms spit out glowing ooze, although no one can figure out why. It's also a mystery why tiny plankton glow when disturbed by storms, waves, and passing boats.

Why do cats usually land on their feet?

Cats are tremendous acrobats. If a cat falls from a short distance, it will almost always land on its feet. Why? Because cats lack collarbones, and can easily rotate and bend their bodies. The backbones of cats are also more flexible than almost any other animal's. All this allows them to turn and land on their feet.

WHY DO CATS COUGH UP HAIR?

Cats groom themselves by licking their fur. Naturally, they end up swallowing some hair in the process. When too much hair collects in a cat's stomach, the stomach lining becomes irritated and—*hack!*—the cat throws up a hairball.

Why do cats meow?

Cats are smart animals—and they communicate with their meows. When things are good, they could be sweetly saying "hello" or "notice me." When they're lonely, stressed or hurt, they often meow a lot to alert you. Hungry cats may sound demanding, while angry cats will sound . . . angry. And when cats get older, they tend to speak more often, possibly to complain of aches and pains.

Why can't
penguins fly?

Long ago, penguins were able to fly. What happened? Swimming happened. Over time, their wings adapted better to their watery environments. Their new flippers allowed for deeper diving for more fish. In fact, some Emperor penguins can dive 1,500 feet (450 meters) and hold their breath for 20 minutes or more. To aid deep sea dives, their bones got denser, and heavier, creating another obstacle to flight.

WHY ARE PENGUINS BLACK AND WHITE?

Penguin feathers are actually camouflage (though they look more like a tuxedo!). When they are swimming, their black back feathers make them hard to see from above. From below, their white chest feathers blend in with the ocean surface, which also makes them hard for predators to spot.

WHY DO EMPEROR PENGUINS HOLD EGGS ON THEIR FEET?

These birds live in a frozen land with no safe place to build a nest. Eggs die if left on the icy ground. So after the females lay the eggs, the males keep the eggs safely off the ice by holding them on the tops of their feet for about 65 days. A layer of skin on the male's stomach hangs down over the egg to keep it warm. After laying the eggs, the females go off to feed. When they return, they are ready for the eggs to hatch. Then it's the male's turn to feast.

13

Why do
ants have antennae?

Like all insects, ants have antennae to help them sense their world. An ant's dangling antennae are super-sensitive. Using them, the ant can follow the scent trails left by other ants. The antennae also help ants feel their way through dark, underground tunnels and identify each other. They're not just for good looks!

Why are some ants called queens?

A human queen leads a country, and an ant queen is the top of the heap in an ant colony. Each ant nest has at least one queen, whose only job is to lay eggs. The more eggs she lays, the more new ants join the nest. All of the other ants have jobs that help the queen.

WHY ARE SOME ANTS CALLED LEAF-CUTTER ANTS?

They get that name from what they do. These ants use their strong jaws to chew through leaves. They are also strong enough to carry pieces of leaves much bigger than themselves. They eat the leaf bits and use them to build nests.

Why do spiders lay so many eggs?

Spiders can lay hundreds of eggs at one time. Some species can produce nearly 2,000 eggs in a single egg sac. Spider eggs and spider babies are very popular meals for many predators. That's why spider mothers have to lay so many eggs—to be sure enough babies live to become adults.

This wolf spider can have more than 1,000 eggs in its protective sac.

WHY DO FEMALE BLACK WIDOW SPIDERS KILL THEIR MATES?

Most people believe the female black widow spider always kills and then eats her mate after mating. This is not always the case. Males often escape the clutches of the female. However, when the female does kill the male, he's her dinner.

What's the difference between **an arachnid and an insect?**

Many people call spiders insects, but they are actually arachnids. Arachnids have eight legs, while insects have only six. Arachnids have eight simple eyes, while insects have two compound eyes. Insects have antennae. Arachnids don't. Unlike most insects, arachnids do not have wings. Besides spiders, other arachnids include scorpions, ticks, and mites.

Why do some animals change color?

Many animals have developed ways to keep from getting eaten. One way is to change color to hide from predators. Animals who do this produce chemicals inside their bodies that change their natural color, often at any time they want. Other animals have hair or skin patterns that blend with each other to confuse predators.

Chameleons can change their colors very quickly.

Why do some animals protect other animals?

Some animals depend on another species to survive. This is called *symbiosis* (sim-by-OH-sis). For example, the tiny clownfish hangs out with the poisonous sea anemone. The clownfish attracts food that the anemone likes to eat in return for the anemone's protection. The anemone's sting, however, does not harm the clownfish.

Zebra stripes make it hard for hungry lions to pick one animal from the herd.

Can you spot the flounder?

Why do squirrels have such **bushy tails?**

When a squirrel is in a tree it uses its big tail for balance. This helps the furry critter to move quickly from branch to branch without falling off. A squirrel's tail keeps the animal warm in the winter; it curls into a ball with the tail as a sort of blanket. The tail also allows the creature to communicate with other squirrels. A squirrel will threaten another squirrel by flinging its tail over its back and flicking it.

WHY DO SQUIRRELS EAT BIRDSEED?

Squirrels will often pounce on a birdfeeder because it is crammed with tasty nuts and seeds. Squirrels are primarily herbivores. They eat plant material such as nuts, fruits, mushrooms, pine cones, leaves, twigs, bark, and yes, birdseed.

DO SQUIRRELS REALLY REMEMBER WHERE THEY HIDE THEIR FOOD?

This famous "fact" about squirrels is a myth: They *don't* always remember where they hide their acorns and chestnuts. Scientists used to believe that squirrels, specifically gray squirrels, remembered where they dug their holes to store their nuts, and also smelled the food they buried. However, studies show that most of the squirrels never recover their buried nuts. In fact, other squirrels find the nuts and keep them. Most acorns and nuts remain buried and grow into young trees.

Why are horses called foals, fillies, mares, colts, and stallions?

A horse is a horse, of course, but different names apply at different times of life. Use this handy chart next time you're at the ranch, the rodeo, or the races:

Colt	A male that's less than 4 years old
Dam	A horse's mother
Filly	A female that's less than 4 years old
Foal	A baby horse
Mare	An adult female that's more than 4 years old
Sire	A horse's father
Stallion	Adult male that's more than 4 years old
Yearling	A horse that is about 1 year old

Why do horses have manes?

Horses are covered with hair all over. The longer hair on their manes—and tails—helps keep bugs and other pests away from the horse's face and neck. Bugs bug horses, too.

WHY ARE HORSES MEASURED IN HANDS?

Thousands of years before anyone knew what inches and feet were, people owned, traded, and sold horses. How could they agree on a horse's size? One measuring device everyone has is a hand. So people started measuring horses by how many hands high it was from the hooves to the shoulder.

Why has being delicious helped the buffalo?

Buffalo (also known as American bison) once lived in enormous herds on the Great Plains. They were hunted so much, they nearly went extinct. In recent years, people have discovered that buffalo meat is low-fat and tender. This has encouraged people to raise them on ranches, helping greatly increase the number of buffalo!

Why do some sheep get painted?

Sheep of the same species all look pretty much alike. So how do you tell which sheep belong to which farm? Farmers can use a safe dye or paint to mark their sheep. It doesn't hurt the sheep and it cuts down on fights between farmers!

Why do goats butt heads?

Sometimes male goats will battle for territory, or for a mate. When they do, they don't have many weapons they can use, so they knock their heads together. Younger males play this way to practice for head-butting battles.

Why do whales **sing**?

The songs of whales, especially humpback whales, can be long, low, and unforgettable. Scientists believe whales sing for a few reasons. They may be looking for a mate. They may be traveling in a new area and want to announce their presence to other whales. It's also been observed that whales sing their sad-sounding songs when they've lost a loved one, or are feeling blue. They are not so different from humans!

Why do musk ox have such **powerful feet and hooves?**

These large animals live in very cold and often frozen lands. Sometimes they have to cut through thick ice in order to find water to drink. They can pound their strong, sharp hooves through the ice for a drink. Those feet are also handy in a fight.

WHY DO LEOPARDS HAVE SPOTS?

Scientists say leopards evolved with dark spots to help them hide from their prey. Cool fact: No two leopards have exactly the same spot pattern.

Why do giraffes have long necks?

Giraffes are the tallest animals on the planet. Some stand up to 19 feet (5.79 m) high. Long necks make it easier to reach leaves high on trees, especially during periods of drought. Long necks are also an advantage in a fight. Male giraffes use their necks as weapons, clubbing their opponents with a heavy skull.

Why do camels have humps?

The humps of camels are filled with fatty tissue. Animals, including humans, store energy in fat. When there's no food or water around, animals live off the stored fat. In the harsh, dry desert, camels' fatty humps help them survive for a long time without water.

Why do birds fly south for the winter?

Some birds—not all—pack their feathers for the winter and fly toward the Equator where it is much warmer. These birds are not only searching for a warmer climate, but are also looking for food and water. Such a journey is known as migration. Before they start their trips, birds stuff themselves with food that becomes fat that they will use as energy for their long journey.

WHY DO BIRDS HAVE FEATHERS?

Feathers keep birds warm, but that's not all they do. Wing feathers help birds fly and steer through the air. Feathers can also be used as camouflage to help a bird hide from predators. Some male birds, such as the peacock, use very colorful feathers to attract a female.

Why do birds sing?

Whether it's the squawk of a crow or the squeak of a cardinal, birds like to sing. Birds hit the high notes because they are communicating with each other. Each birdcall has a different meaning. Sometimes males sing to attract a female. Other times, a male is warning other birds to keep away from his nest. Birds also warn each other when predators, such as hawks or cats, approach.

Why do caterpillars spin cocoons?

When is a caterpillar not a caterpillar? When it is a butterfly. Caterpillars turn into butterflies through a process called metamorphosis (met-ah-MOR-fa-sis). There are four stages of a butterfly's metamorphosis. The first stage is when the adult female butterfly lays her eggs. A caterpillar is a larva that hatches from one of the eggs. Caterpillars have only one job—to eat as much as possible. When caterpillars are fully grown, they stop eating. Then they spin a cocoon. This is called the pupa stage. The pupa of a butterfly is called a chrysalis. The pupa hangs on a branch or a leaf. Inside the cocoon, the caterpillar completely changes into the adult stage—a butterfly that ultimately breaks out of the cocoon and flies away.

Why are moths attracted to light?

Moonlight helps moths navigate—they use the moon to orient themselves. When they spot an artificial light, such as your porch light, they get confused and begin to circle around that light, ignoring the moonlight.

WHY DO CICADAS BUZZ?

When summer rolls around, listen carefully. You might hear the buzz of the cicada, which sounds like an electric razor. Cicadas are insects that resemble huge flies. They buzz to attract a mate. The sound is produced by a pair of drum-like organs on the base of their abdomen. These organs vibrate at high speed, creating a buzzing sound that you can usually hear between mid-July and September.

EARTH

Why are hurricane winds so powerful?

Page 28

25

Why is Earth a Goldilocks Planet?

Of all the planets in our Solar System, only Earth has known life on it. That's because our planet orbits in what scientists call the Goldilocks Zone— the distance from the sun that creates temperatures that are not too hot or too cold to support life. The Earth has a breathable atmosphere, too. Everything is "just right." Scientists are looking around the galaxy for other planets in this zone—we might not be alone!

WHY CAN TARDIGRADES LIVE IN OUTER SPACE?

Tardigrades—sometimes called *water bears*—are adorable microscopic creatures that can survive extreme cold, heat, and pressure. They can be frozen and brought back to life, all of which explains how some tardigrades have survived in outer space. Creatures that can live in extreme places and temperatures are called *extremophiles*. They might offer a clue to how life could exist on other planets.

Why do we need the Earth to spin?

The Earth spins completely around its axis once every 24 hours. Sound familiar? The spinning of the Earth creates the day and night cycles that many plants and animals need to survive. The spinning motion also helps keep ocean currents moving, shapes cloud and weather systems, and keeps the magnetic field around the Earth safe and sound.

Why do tornadoes happen?

A tornado is a column of rapidly rotating air that generally begins as a thunderstorm. The atmosphere becomes unstable when warm, moist air bangs into a wall of cool, dry air. Warm air near the ground rises, cold air in the upper atmosphere falls. A tornado spins when the wind's speed and direction cause the rising air to rotate vertically in the middle of the storm.

WHY DOES TORNADO ALLEY GET SO MANY TORNADOES?

Tornado Alley is found in the central United States, roughly between Texas and North Dakota. Although tornadoes occur throughout the U.S., they take place more often and with more force in Tornado Alley. Why? Tornado Alley is flat. It is also where warm, moist air from the Gulf of Mexico and cold, dry air from Canada collide. When that happens, tornadoes are born.

WHY ARE TORNADOES DANGEROUS?

Tornadoes are storms of swirling wind that are among the most violent in nature. Tornadoes can generate wind speeds of 250 mph (402 km) or higher. As they move, tornadoes can cut a path of destruction a mile wide and more than 50 miles (80 km) long. Once a tornado picked up a motel sign in Oklahoma and dropped it 30 miles (48 km) away, in Arkansas.

Why can astronauts see the Grand Canyon from space?

The Grand Canyon is more than a big hole in the ground. It is a wonder of nature. The canyon is 277 miles (446 km) long, up to 18 miles (29 km) wide, and one mile (1.6 km) deep. The rushing water of the Colorado River carved out the canyon over millions of years. The Grand Canyon is so huge that astronauts can see it from space without a telescope.

WHY DOES THE GRAND CANYON GET SO COLD AT NIGHT?

The Grand Canyon is in the desert. During a summer day, the bottom of the canyon can get extremely hot, with temperatures reaching more than 100°F (38°C). In more humid environments, moisture in the air filters sunlight before it reaches the ground, and traps heat at night. Deserts have very dry air, which holds little moisture. As soon as the sun sets, the air cools, especially at the rim of the canyon, causing a big temperature drop.

Why is the Grand Canyon colorful?

The layers of rock in the Grand Canyon formed over millions of years. Each layer reflects the conditions that were present when it was created, and so each looks slightly different from the others, creating colorful stripes of reds, browns, and oranges.

Lava can get as hot as 2,200°F (1,204°C).

WHY CAN A VOLCANO CHANGE THE WEATHER?

Volcanoes spew out more than lava. After an eruption, huge black clouds of ash might fill the air for thousands of miles. These massive clouds can block sunlight from reaching the Earth, which can cause lower temperatures and changes in rainfall.

Why do volcanoes erupt?

Imagine a soda can. Shake the can, and gas and pressure build up inside. Open the top and *bam!*—an explosion occurs. Volcanoes work much the same way. The heat deep inside Earth is so intense that it melts rock and creates explosive gases. Scientists call that molten rock magma. Magma slowly rises to the surface, collecting in underground chambers. Eventually, the pressure of the magma becomes so great that it pushes through Earth's crust. Soon a volcano is blowing its top.

WHY IS LAVA HOT?

Temperatures inside the earth can reach more than 2,000°F (1,100°C). Magma is rock that has melted in that heat. It is called lava when it flows above ground. As lava cools and hardens at the surface, it can still be hot enough to burn or even kill a person.

Why do **earthquakes** **destroy** some **buildings** and not others?

During an earthquake, the ground shakes, twists, and heaves, causing buildings to move. Houses can shift on their foundations, crack, and tumble to the ground. Some buildings, however, are built to withstand violent earthquakes. The buildings in the back of this photo were braced with special materials to keep them standing.

WHY ARE EARTHQUAKES MEASURED ON THE RICHTER SCALE?

Scientists needed a way to record information after an earthquake and compare it to other events. In 1935, Dr. Charles Richter developed a system that measured the strength of an earthquake on a scale from 0 to 10, with a twist—each number is 10 times greater than the one before it. So, a deadly 7.0 caused 10 times more motion than a 6.0 magnitude quake.

Why are hurricane winds so powerful?

Hurricanes have winds that blow at least 74 miles (119 km) per hour. Those winds are fueled by warm ocean water. When a storm passes over the warm water, the strong rotational movement of Earth causes the moist air over the ocean to spiral upward. Those spirals move faster and faster as the energy builds, creating hurricane-force winds. The energy from the heat of the water also adds power to the wind.

WHY IS IT EASIER TO FLOAT IN THE OCEAN?

Salt in the ocean makes the water denser, or thicker, than fresh water. The denser the water, the easier it is to float on it.

Why is the ocean salty?

Ocean water gets its salt from rocks on land. When rain falls, it erodes the rocks. The water dissolves minerals from the rocks, including chloride and sodium, which are the main ingredients in salt. Those minerals flow down streams and rivers into the ocean.

Why shouldn't I drink salt water?

First, it tastes pretty bad. Second, it causes dehydration. If you drank salt water, your body would have to get rid of more water than you drank in order to filter out the extra salt. As a result, you would be thirstier than before you drank the salt water.

31

Why is the **atmosphere important?**

Earth's atmosphere is made up of several layers of gases surrounding the planet. The outer layers of the atmosphere protect us from many things, including the sun's harmful rays. The sun bathes Earth in ultraviolet radiation that can damage our eyes and skin. The atmosphere's ozone layer absorbs much of this radiation.

Mesosphere: 31-53 miles (50-85 km)

Stratosphere: 9-31 miles (14.5-50 km)

Troposphere: 5-9 miles (8-14.5 km)

Why are **air and oxygen different?**

While oxygen is the most important gas in the atmosphere for people, it's not all we breathe. Earth's air is actually 78 percent nitrogen, plus 21 percent oxygen. The remaining 1 percent is carbon dioxide (what we breathe out), a bit of a gas called argon, and tiny amounts of other gases, plus some water vapor.

WHY IS IT MORE DIFFICULT TO BREATHE AT HIGHER ALTITUDES?

At high altitudes, 1 mile (1.61 km) or more above sea level, the air is thinner. Air pressure decreases the higher you go. For your lungs to fill with breathable air, the air pressure in your lungs has to be less than the pressure of the air outside. When it's not, breathing becomes strained.

Why are **space rockets so fast?**

To leave earth's atmosphere and travel the full 60 miles (96 km) to space, rockets have to fight the mighty force of gravity. The speed to accomplish that— called *escape velocity*—is calculated for each size and type of rocket that is sent up. A rocket launching a space shuttle needs to reach 7 miles per second (11 kps), or more than 25,200 miles per hour (40,555 kph), to enter orbit.

Why can spacecraft help Earth?

From space, satellites and spacecraft can take photos and video of as much as half of Earth in one shot. Scientists study those images to learn about weather patterns, ocean currents, and erosion. The information we receive helps us get the big picture back on Earth.

Earth is 25,000 miles (40,234 km) around and it makes one full spin in 24 hours.

33

Why do some people wear **surgical masks outdoors?**

In some large cities, pollution is very bad. The air can be thick with smoke and tiny particles of soot. Such pollution can be annoying or even dangerous. Surgical masks can act as an air filter. During cold and flu season, some people also wear masks to keep germs in . . . or out.

Why can't we see air?

Air is all around us, but we can't see it. That's because Earth's atmosphere is made up of gases. The molecules of these gases don't reflect light that our eyes can see, so air is invisible to us.

WHY DOES HOT AIR CAUSE A BALLOON TO RISE?

When air is heated, its molecules move faster. The faster the molecules move, the more space they have between them. This means that hot air is less dense than cold air, so the hot air floats on top of the cold air, causing the balloon to rise. When the air inside the balloon cools, the balloon goes down.

Why do clouds have different shapes?

Clouds form when heated air rises. As it slowly cools, water vapor condenses into visible droplets, forming a cloud. Wind and temperature patterns push the cloud formations into different shapes. A cloud's shape can be a clue to help cloud-watchers predict what weather is ahead.

Cumulonimbus clouds are the big storm makers. Enormous tops float above dark clouds closer to the surface.

Cumulus clouds are the fluffiest. They build when winds are light and weather is fair.

Cirrus clouds are thin and wispy and almost transparent. They can clearly show wind direction.

Stratus clouds are heavy and wide, usually because they are filled with rain just before a storm.

Why does the ocean have waves?

Winds create waves on oceans and lakes. When the wind blows, it transfers some of its energy to the water. Friction between the air molecules and water molecules creates a wave. That's true of most waves on the surface of the ocean, too. Ocean waves are made larger by the transfer of energy from storms, which move larger amounts of water.

WHY DO TIDES FORM?

Tides form when the moon's gravitational pull tugs on Earth's oceans. When that happens, the sea rises toward the moon. High tides occur on the side of the Earth facing the moon. Low tides occur on the side of Earth facing away from the moon.

Why are tsunamis so dangerous?

Tsunamis are monster ocean waves caused by underwater disturbances such as earthquakes, volcanic eruptions, or landslides. The energy created by these events spreads outward from the epicenter. Large volumes of water, known as swells, also move from the center. The swells become high waves as they bunch up in shallow water near the shore. By the time they reach shore, the monster waves might have grown as high as 100 feet (30.5 m).

Why do people sink in quicksand?

Quicksand is an ordinary mixture of sand and clay that becomes water-logged. Such a mushy mixture cannot support weight. Quicksand itself won't suck you down, but you can get stuck in it. Moving will cause you to sink deeper. But don't despair—quicksand is generally only a few feet deep. How do you get out of quicksand? The best thing to do is to move slowly. If you struggle, you'll sink. If you relax and try to lie on your back, you can get yourself out of this mess.

Danger
Quick sand

Keep away

Danger
Quarry workings

Why is soil mostly **brown**?

Soil is created by plants and animals decomposing. Over time, dead trees, flowers, and even bits of food break down into a substance called humus, which makes the soil look brown. Sometimes soil is red, yellow, or even black, depending on the organic material and minerals in the area. Red soil, for example, contains a lot of iron.

WHY DO SINKHOLES FORM?

When rock under the soil dissolves, it can leave huge spaces underground. Suddenly, the soil collapses—and a sinkhole is born. Sinkholes come in various sizes. They are mainly caused by water circulating underground, which breaks up the surrounding rock. Some sinkholes are big enough to swallow cars or buildings.

Why is the Earth's climate changing?

Over the last hundred years, humans have used more and more factories, cars, engines, and other machines. That creates a lot of smoke, heat, and other pollution that builds up inside our atmosphere. These particles and gases trap heat as it radiates from the Earth, causing temperatures to rise. Over time, this has affected the climate. Storms and droughts are becoming worse, and summers are becoming hotter. Melting ice caps are causing ocean levels to slowly rise, flooding low coastal areas. Scientists around the world are warning us: Make changes—fast—or things will get worse.

Why are Earth's ice caps melting?

The heat is on in Antarctica and the Arctic. Global warming, an overall rise in Earth's temperature, is melting the polar ice caps. That is causing huge chunks of Antarctic ice to fall into the ocean. In the Arctic, the icy territories where polar bears live are melting, threatening these beautiful bears.

Metamorphic Rock

Why does Earth have different **types of rocks?**

Earth rocks! While there are many different types of rocks on the planet, they fall into only three categories: igneous, metamorphic, and sedimentary. Igneous rocks, such as pumice, form when molten rock reaches Earth's surface and cools. Metamorphic rocks, such as marble, are created when igneous or sedimentary rock changes, or metamorphoses, as a result of temperature, pressure, or stress. Sedimentary rocks, such as sandstone, form when sediments build up and are compacted together by Earth's powerful forces.

Sedimentary Rock

Igneous Rock

Why are **diamonds** so rare?

Diamonds form when carbon deep below Earth's surface is squeezed under tremendous pressure. Diamonds are rare because pressure seldom pushes the gems to the surface. Only 500 tons (453,592 kg) of diamonds have ever been mined. Meanwhile, more than 300 times more gold has been found!

SPACE

Why do astronauts spend months in the Space Station?

Page 45

41

Why does Earth have ?

Scientists have scratched their heads for centuries trying to figure out where the moon came from. Many now believe an object about the size of Mars slammed into Earth a long time ago. That crash sent a huge chunk of Earth into outer space where it began orbiting the planet as our moon. Earth's gravitational pull keeps the moon in place.

Why is the surface of the moon like cocoa powder?

When astronauts first reached the moon in 1969, they tramped through soft powder with each step. The moon's powder is made of . . . glass? Yes. Meteoroids have smashed into the moon over millions of years in places, and the collisions created enough heat to turn some of the minerals into glass. This glass was ground down by more collisions, and the result is a soft, clingy powder similar to cocoa powder, but not as tasty.

SOLAR SYSTEM WEIGH-IN

Because other planets have different gravity, things weigh less or more on them than they do on Earth. Here's how much a 100-pound (45-kg) person would weigh if standing on each of these planets (and our sun and moon). Where would you like to go first?

	Pounds	Kg		Pounds	Kg
Mercury	38	17	Jupiter	236	107
Venus	91	41	Saturn	92	42
Earth	100	45	Uranus	90	40
Moon	17	8	Neptune	112	51
Mars	38	17	Sun	2,801	1,270

Why are there are seas on the moon?

Hundreds of years ago, early telescopes allowed scientists their first close look at the moon. Those astronomers saw wide, flat areas that looked like oceans or seas. Even though they were later found to have no water, many areas of the Moon today still have *Mare* (which means sea) as part of their name. For example, one crater is called Mare Nectaris, which means Sea of Nectar!

WHY DOES THE MOON HAVE CRATERS?

Asteroids and meteoroids have often smashed into the moon's surface, causing craters. Unlike Earth, the moon does not have a protective atmosphere, which would burn up most falling objects before they struck the ground.

Why do we have blood moons?

During a total lunar eclipse, the shadow of the Earth blocks the moon for a while. At that time, the only light that reaches the moon is filtered through the earth's atmosphere. That causes the light to take on an orange or reddish color, much like a sunset.

Why do we have blue moons?

A blue moon occurs when there are two full moons in the same month. Blue moons don't happen that often, which is why the phrase "once in a blue moon" refers to something that is rare.

Why do we call Mars the
Red Planet ?

We should really call Mars the Rusty Planet. Its soil is rich in iron oxides, known to Earthlings as rust. Iron oxides are chemical compounds, made up of iron and oxygen, that are a reddish color. Some ancient people used to think that blood caused the reddish glow of Mars.

Why are there canals on Mars?

Although many people used to think that Mars had canals, that's not the case. Giovanni Schiaparelli, an Italian astronomer, first spotted straight lines on the planet's surface in 1877. He called those lines *canali*. In Italian, *canali* means "channels" or "grooves." However, people mistakenly translated the word into English as "canals." Some people even claimed Martians built the "canals." The canals are optical illusions caused by craters and other surface features. When Mars is viewed through today's stronger telescopes, the canals disappear.

The deepest canyon on Mars is 4.97 mi (8 km) de...

Why are **satellites** sent into space?

Since the launch of Sputnik in 1957, thousands of artificial satellites have been sent into orbit by government agencies and commercial enterprises. They circle our planet, forecast weather over wide areas, take photos, and bounce radio, TV, phone, and Internet signals from one part of Earth to another.

Why do astronauts **spend months** in the Space Station?

Now that humans have reached the moon, the next goal is space travel to other planets. To learn how humans adapt to life in space, astronauts from several countries have spent many months orbiting Earth in the International Space Station. They perform experiments and study the human body's reactions to weightlessness. They are the pioneers of future space travel.

Why is the sun so bright?

The sun is a big ball of super-heated gas that sends 44 quadrillion watts of energy to the Earth's surface every year. (It would take 44 million large power plants to produce that much energy in a year!) The sun gets its enormous energy through fusion, a nuclear reaction that joins together the nuclei of atoms. Fusion takes place deep inside the sun at searing temperatures of 27 million°F (15 million°C). Fusion converts hydrogen to helium and releases energy, which makes the sun very bright and able to give off so much light and heat.

WHY IS OUR SUN A YELLOW DWARF?

The life of a star is very long, but like any life, it has stages. For a star the size of our sun, that life cycle starts as a protostar. In about two billion years, it grows in energy and size and becomes a yellow dwarf, which our sun is now. In about five billion more years, the sun will expand and become a red giant. As its energy decreases, it will shrink and become a white dwarf. When the sun dies, in 6 billion years, it will be a black stellar corpse.

Why does the sun have spots?

Sunspots are relatively cool areas on the sun's surface. The spots are about 8,132°F (4,500°C). They are created when strong magnetic fields rise from the sun's interior to the surface. These magnetic fields interrupt the normal process that brings energy to the sun's surface and makes it bright and hot. Sunspots can be as large as 50,000 miles (80,000 km) wide.

Why don't **planets orbit in perfect circles?**

Planets revolve around the sun in elliptical, or oval-like orbits, also known as eccentric orbits. The sun's gravitational pull tugs the planets toward it, while each planet's forward momentum tries to keep it moving in a straight line. This planetary tug-of-war causes an elliptical orbit.

WHY DOES OUR SOLAR SYSTEM MOVE?

Everything in space is in motion. Our moon orbits Earth, which orbits our sun. The sun, at the center of our solar system, is also in orbit around the center of the Milky Way galaxy—at a speed of 515,000 miles per hour (829,000 kph). It takes 230 million years for our solar system to complete one orbit.

Why did people once believe **the sun revolved around Earth?**

Everyone from the ancient Greeks up through people living in the Middle Ages, which lasted until 1500 A.D., believed Earth was the center of the universe. They believed the sun, the moon, and the planets revolved around Earth because seeing is believing . . . and from Earth, it looks like Earth is in the center. In 1543, an astronomer named Nicolas Copernicus determined the Earth and the planets revolved around the sun. In 1610, Galileo Galilei, an Italian astronomer, used a telescope to prove that Copernicus was right.

Why isn't Pluto a regular planet anymore?

A planet is an object that orbits a sun and has enough mass that gravity shapes it into a sphere. Once upon a time, Pluto was the smallest, coldest, and least understood planet in our solar system. Many people said Pluto shouldn't be a planet at all. They believed Pluto was too small—just a chunk of ice beyond the orbit of Neptune. In 2006, the International Astronomical Union (IAU) formally downgraded Pluto, calling it a dwarf planet, which is smaller than a regular planet.

Why was the New Horizons spacecraft a scientific first?

Launched in January 2006, New Horizons whizzed by Pluto, 4.67 billion miles (7.5 billion km) from Earth, in July 2015. No other spacecraft has ever come so close to the dwarf planet. The pictures and data New Horizons sent back showed that Pluto has high mountains (right), wide ice fields (toward top of image), and even a thin atmosphere. So many pictures are being sent back, it will be years before the research is completed.

Why are some planets called gas giants?

Saturn, Jupiter, Neptune, and Uranus are not hard, rocky places like Earth or Mars. They have small, hard cores at their center, but surrounding their cores are thousands of miles of thick gases. When the planets were forming, all that gas was pulled in by the core's gravity. Over millions of years, the gas layers got thicker and thicker, making these four planets the largest in our solar system.

Why do our largest planets have so many moons?

Larger planets have stronger gravity. That powerful pulling force attracts larger objects into their orbits in a way smaller planets cannot. That's why our solar system's two largest planets boast the most moons: Jupiter has 67 and Saturn has 62, of which 53 have been officially named.

THE RINGS AROUND SATURN AND OTHER PLANETS ARE MOSTLY ROCKS IN ORBIT.

When small moons and comets get too close to a planet, gravity rips them apart. Bits of rocks and ice begin orbiting the planet, often colliding with each other so they cannot come together into larger bodies. This floating dust and ice creates rings.

Why do galaxies have different shapes?

Galaxies contain hundreds of billions of stars, and come in three shapes: spiral, elliptical, and irregular. Our galaxy, the Milky Way, is a spiral. Galaxies can be shaped by many different forces, including centrifugal force (which pushes objects on a circular path outward), collisions with other galaxies, and gravity. Over billions of years, the shape of each galaxy will keep changing.

Why can't we see the center of the Milky Way?

Our solar system is way out on the edge of the Milky Way. Solar systems, gas clouds, and other objects lie between Earth and the galaxy's core, creating a milky-looking haze that is difficult to see through. Scientists believe that there is a supermassive black hole at the center of the galaxy.

WHY CAN WE SEE SOME GALAXIES WITHOUT TELESCOPES?

We can see two of the Milky Way's closest neighboring galaxies—the Magellanic Clouds—without the help of telescopes because they are so bright. The clouds appear in the Southern Hemisphere and are named after the 16th century explorer Ferdinand Magellan.

Why does the **North Star stay in the same position?**

The North Star, or Polaris, lines up with Earth's northern axis. Like the center of a carousel, Polaris is a constant. As Earth spins, Polaris does not move from its position. This time-lapse photo shows the stars moving around Polaris at the center.

WHY DO THE CONSTELLATIONS MOVE ACROSS THE SKY?

Because the Earth spins, we seem to see the stars rise and set, just as we see the sun and moon rise and set. Over the course of a year, the earth also moves around the sun, causing different constellations to be overhead at different times of the year.

Why are **comets so predictable?**

Comets orbit the sun just as planets do. However, a comet's orbit is usually much longer and wider than a planet's. Just as scientists know when Mars or Saturn will be visible in their orbits, they can predict a comet's arrival very precisely. For instance, on July 28, 2061, the famous Halley's comet will pass Earth for the first time in 75 years.

Comet 103P/Hartley 2

Mars

Earth

Venus

Mercury

9/14/2010
9/30/2010
11/04/2010
11/30/2010
12/12/2010

Why are asteroids different sizes?

Asteroids are chunks of rock and metal that orbit the sun. Asteroids play a cosmic game of football as they continually smack into one another. The collisions change their shapes and sizes. The largest asteroid appears to be Ceres, which is 565 miles (909 km) long. The smaller asteroids are just a few feet in size. Some are small particles loosely bound together. Others are pieces of solid rock.

WHY ARE THERE ASTEROID BELTS?

People once thought asteroid belts formed when planets exploded. Now, scientists believe asteroids are rocks that never formed into a planet. The closest asteroid belt contains hundreds of thousands of asteroids. It lies between the orbits of Mars and Jupiter.

Why do astronomers measure **distances** in **light years?**

Because outer space is so vast, astronomers use a measurement far, far greater than miles or kilometers. A light year is the amount of time it takes light to travel (in a vacuum) in one year—roughly 5.88 trillion miles (9.46 trillion km). Even at that great size, we often measure objects millions of light years away.

Why can't we travel at the speed of light?

If the spaceship of the future could travel at the speed of light, it would move 186,000 miles (300,000 km) per second, or 670 million miles (1,079 million km) per hour.
At that speed you would get to the moon in 1.2 seconds.
We can't travel at the speed of light because such a speed would take more energy than we are able to generate.

Albert Einstein said we could travel through time.

HUMANS

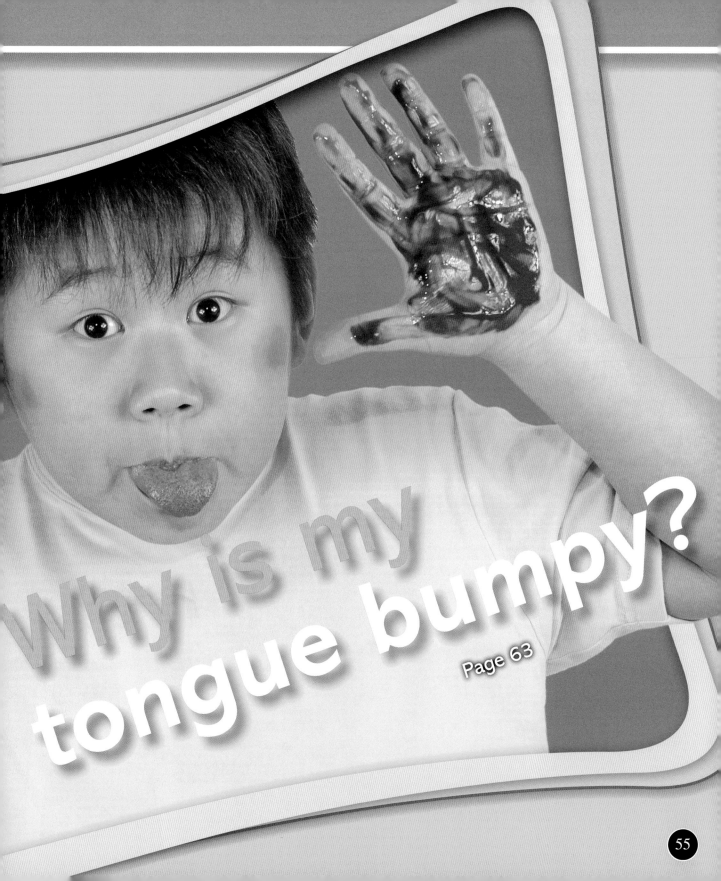

Why is my tongue bumpy?

Page 63

55

Why are some people taller than others?

Your height is usually influenced by the height of your parents and their parents. Height and other physical traits such as eye color, hair color, and skin color are passed along to you in your genes. Genes determine many things about you, including how much growth hormone your body produces, and how big your bones get. Your diet, where you live, and your overall health also help decide how tall you'll be, but your parents are the main factor.

WHY ARE THERE DIFFERENT SKIN COLORS?

Your skin color is determined by the amount of a pigment called melanin in your skin. Melanin is a chemical that protects the skin from the sun's ultraviolet rays. People with light or fair complexions have less melanin in their skin than people with darker skin tones.

Freckles are more common in people with light skin.

Why do some kids have freckles?

Sometimes melanin is produced in the skin in clumps instead of being evenly distributed. That causes freckles. Some freckles are tan colored, others are light brown and very small. Because exposure to sunlight causes the skin to produce more melanin, freckles usually fade in the wintertime. People who want to avoid getting freckles should stay out of the sun.

Why do some people have birthmarks?

Not surprisingly, birthmarks are skin marks people are born with. There are two main types of birthmarks. One type, called *vascular*, occurs when tiny blood vessels grow in one concentrated area. These make the skin pink, red, or purple. The other type, called *pigmented*, happen when there is more pigment (color) in one part of the skin. These birthmarks can be light brown, black, or even blue-gray. Moles can be birthmarks, too.

WHY DO PEOPLE HAVE MOLES?

Moles are a collection of cells that contain color. People often refer to them as beauty marks. Moles are not painful but if they change size, shape, or color, talk to a doctor.

Why do some men go bald?

There are many reasons that people go bald, but the most common is caused by genes and hormones. Each hair grows from a follicle on your head. In some men, the follicles close up, so they no longer grow hair. If you are a guy and your mother's father went bald, you have a greater chance of going bald yourself!

WHY DO SOME PEOPLE HAVE MORE HAIR THAN OTHERS?

Genes and hormones determine whether someone can grow a lot of hair. For some people, hair grows easily. For others, it comes in slowly and is very thin. Usually, the hair on a person's head grows at a rate of about half an inch (13 mm) every month.

Why does hair turn gray?

Every strand of hair has a root that keeps it anchored in place. The root is surrounded by a follicle under the skin. Each follicle has pigment (color) cells that produce a chemical called melanin, which gives hair its color. As a person gets older the pigment cells die off. When that happens, the hair no longer contains as much melanin. That causes it to turn gray or white.

Why do knuckles crack?

Knuckles are the joints in the fingers where two bones meet. Each of your body's joints is surrounded by a case of thick, clear liquid that keeps the cartilage, tissues, and muscles lubricated and nourished. Inside that liquid you'll find gases, such as oxygen, nitrogen, and carbon dioxide. When you bend your fingers, you stretch the case around the joint, which increases the amount of fluid. When that happens, the bubbles in the fluid begin to burst, producing the cracking noise that makes people crazy!

WHY DO OUR EYES TWITCH?

A twitching eye can really be annoying. It can happen when you're reading a book or talking to a friend. Researchers say a twitching eye is caused by muscle spasms in the eyelid. These spasms may be brought on by stress or physical eyestrain.

Don't be so sure that person is winking at you!

Why is some hair curly?

Hair grows from your head one strand at a time. In many people, those strands are long and straight. However, for other people, the strands start to turn around and around almost as soon as they start growing out of the head, which can result in some *seriously* curly hair.

Why do we cry?

We cry when we are sad, or when we are hurt. It's nature's way of showing something is wrong. Not all tears are emotional, however. We cry when we peel onions, because the gas released by onions irritates them. And when our eyes are tired—the eyes dry out and the tears keep them moist.

WHY DO I GET TEARS WHEN I'M NOT CRYING?

There are three types of tears. Basal tears are the first type. They act as a protective barrier between the eye and the rest of the world. Next are reflex tears. They wash your eyes clean when something gets in them. Finally, there are emotional tears.

Why do we get crusty stuff in the corners of our eyes?

Some people call them eye boogers, gunk, sand, or sleep. Whatever the term, that's the crusty stuff that gathers in the corners of our eyes, especially after sleeping. The official name is *rheum* (pronounced "room"). It's mucus, oil, and skin cells that naturally seep from both eyes. As rheum dries overnight, it collects in the corners of our eyes and greets us in the morning!

Why are some people color blind?

Most people's eyes have retinas made up of small parts called cones and rods. Rods help people see in low light, while cones allow people to see objects in color. Each cone has a different pigment, which helps a person tell the difference between colors. The eyes of color blind people are usually missing certain cones. So they might see colors, but not the right ones. What does that mean? For example, to some color-blind people, green vegetables look brown, while red and green traffic lights look almost the same. They might even have trouble matching the color of their clothes.

If you can't see this number, you might be color blind.

Why are eyes different colors?

Eyes are very similar to skin—their coloring depends on a pigment called melanin. Each person's genes determine how much melanin they have. People with a lot of melanin have brown eyes, those with hardly any have blue, and green lies somewhere in between. So whether you have baby blues, big browns, or glorious green eyes, thank the melanin—and your parents, from whom you inherited it all.

Molars

Premolars

Canines

Incisors

Why do I have different kinds of teeth?

Different teeth have different jobs. You have sharp incisors at the very front to cut off pieces of food. Then comes another set of sharp teeth called canines. Next to them, your premolars are flatter, to help smush your food. The big molars in the back do the heavy grinding, softening the food until it's ready to swallow. That's quite a mouthful!

Why do baby teeth fall out?

Most adult teeth are too large to fit in a kid's mouth. So kids have smaller "baby" teeth that do the job until their jaws grow big enough to support stronger adult teeth. As children grow, their adult teeth slowly push the baby teeth out.

Why can we whistle?

Blowing air through your pursed lips causes the air to vibrate, which creates sound waves. Your mouth serves as a resonance chamber, much like the body of a guitar or violin, bouncing the sound waves around and making them louder. Most people whistle this way. Others can whistle through their fingers or cupped hands.

WHY ARE LIPS RED?

Lips are red because the skin covering them is thin. We can see the blood vessels, known as capillaries, located just below that thin skin.

Why is my tongue bumpy?

The tiny bumps and ridges in your tongue have an important job: they taste your food. Taste buds cover most of your tongue, and they help your body know what you're putting in your mouth. These buds will let you know when something tastes good, but they also provide warning when something tastes bad—or is even dangerous.

63

Why do we need food?

Your body needs food the way a car needs gas. Food is your fuel: it gives you energy and nutrition to grow, move, and be healthy. By giving your body the proper amounts of nutrients and energy, you're giving yourself a better chance to stay healthy.

WHY DO SOME PEOPLE CRAVE JUNK FOOD?

Some researchers say that people can become addicted to sugar, salt, and fat—the three ingredients that make junk food taste so good. One study found that a diet high in fat changes the brain's biochemistry in the same way that drugs can. When your body is used to eating overly fatty foods, it does not feel full after eating low-fat foods. In another study, rats were only fed food that was very high in sugar. When sugar was taken away from those rats, they had chattering teeth and shaking bodies, signifying a junk food crash!

WHY IS EXERCISE IMPORTANT?

Exercise burns calories and helps you stay trim and fit. It can also help you relax, reduce stress, and keep your organs, such as your heart and lungs, healthy.

Yoga is an enjoyable an effective way to exercise.

Why do we **need** to eat a variety of foods?

Your body needs many different nutrients and chemicals to stay strong and healthy. However, not even vegetables contain all the nutrition your body demands. That's why you need a diet that includes foods from many groups. This handy chart shows you a good way to plan your balanced diet.

Fruits

Fruits help guard against some diseases, and also have fiber that helps your digestion. Plus, they're nature's original candy. Sweet!

Grains

Grains give you energy, and whole grains don't have much fat—making whole grains a great power food that can have lots of fiber.

Vegetables

Your tongue may disagree, but the rest of your body wants veggies. With so many vitamins and other nutrients, vegetables should be the biggest portion on your plate.

Dairy

Dairy includes milk, cheese, and yogurt. Dairy is good for you, but not in large amounts.

Protein

Meat, nuts, beans, and eggs are some of the best ways to get energy into your diet. Eating lean meats is a good way to keep trim, too.

Why does a hot pepper
burn my tongue?

If you've ever bitten into a jalapeño or a chili pepper, you probably felt the burn. Hot peppers contain a stinging substance called *capsaicin* (cap-SAY-sin). It's the pepper plant's natural defense against animals that might want to eat it.

WHY DO I GET "BRAIN FREEZE"?

When you toss back a frozen drink or an ice cream cone, that sudden cold temperature surprises your brain. Your brain sends you that well-known pain sensation to tell you to slow down. So take your time and avoid the freeze!

Thank you, Joseph Fry. This British inventor created the first chocolate bar in 1847!

Why does chocolate make me hyper?

Chocolate contains sugar and caffeine. It's the caffeine, not the sugar, that really makes a person jumpy. Caffeine sends a jolt to your nervous system and brain, making you more awake and alert. Meanwhile, the sugar goes into your bloodstream to provide a short burst of physical energy and releases a chemical in your brain that makes you feel good. It also makes you want to keep eating that sugary food. However, the sugar gets used up quickly, often leaving you to wonder where all of that energy went.

WHY DOES SODA MAKE ME BURP?

Do you call it soda or pop? Either way, what makes that drink fizzy is a gas called carbon dioxide. When you crack open a can or bottle, you're drinking a lot of bubbles along with that sweet soda. Your body doesn't want all that gas, so it just might send it back out—in a long, loud, roof-shaking burp.

Why is mother's milk so good for babies?

Mother's milk is naturally produced for human babies to help them thrive and stay healthy. It provides nutrients and important disease-fighting ingredients. And it's very easy to digest!

Why do I make spit?

Spit, more politely called *saliva*, is made up mostly of water and other proteins. Saliva helps keep your mouth clean and your tongue wet. It is also the first step of digestion, breaking down starches in your food before it travels to your stomach. Even though you may produce several pints of saliva each day, spit is way too valuable to splatter on the sidewalk!

Spit helps you swallow food.

WHY DOES PUS FORM ON A CUT?

When skin is punctured or cut, bacteria make their way into the body. The body's white blood cells, which fight off infection, rush to the scene of the injury. Sometimes bacteria overwhelm the disease-fighting white blood cells. When that happens, they call for help. Pus is what you get when millions of white blood cells tackle the bacteria.

Why do I cough up mucus when I'm sick?

When you have a cold, your respiratory system produces gunk called *phlegm* (flem). Your body produces this sticky goo to fight off invading viruses and bacteria. After the phlegm has done its job, your body tries to get rid of it by coughing. If that doesn't work, the phlegm can build up, becoming thicker and sometimes green.

Why do I get a runny nose?

When you have a cold virus or you are allergic to something, your body's defenses try to get the virus out. One way is to mix the virus into mucus and send it out through your nose. So grab a tissue and start blowing!

WHY DO I HAVE BOOGERS?

Booger is the slang term we give to dried or lumpy nasal mucus. If you think of your nose as a vacuum cleaner, you can imagine it sucking in bits of dirt and dust every day. Your nose hair is the filter that traps those unwanted particles. Gooey mucus surrounds the dirt, forming slimy lumps to stop that stuff from getting into your lungs. When people blow or pick their noses, they remove all that junk from their noses. And if they eat it, they put all that trapped dirt back into their body!

Why do I have earwax?

Earwax isn't good for making candles, but it does have a brilliant job. It helps the body defend against unwanted invaders. Earwax traps dirt and bacteria that would otherwise get into your body through the ears. Think of it as boogers for your ears!

Why does my stomach growl after I eat?

Everything is quiet and suddenly—rrrrumble—someone's stomach starts making a grumbling, rumbling, or sloshing noise. That noise is made by the stomach's muscles. The digestive system is pushing a gooey mixture of food and liquid through the digestive tract. Traveling along with all that mush is air and gas, which gets squeezed. And when anything filled with gas gets a squeeze, noises are sure to follow.

Why do farts smell bad?

Everybody passes gas. In fact, the average person passes gas 14 times a day. (And we all know people who are way above average.) Where does that gas come from? When you swallow air along with your food, it usually comes back up as a burp. But some of that gas passes on from your stomach to your intestines. Other gas is formed in the digestive tract, where your poop is being created. Not surprisingly, it smells pretty bad in there. To ease the pressure and let those gases out, your body expels it through your exhaust pipe—otherwise known as the rectum.

WHY DO I HAVE TO THROW UP SOMETIMES?

When your stomach realizes that something's in there that doesn't belong, it sends that foreign substance back where it came from. Sometimes it's bad food, sometimes you've got a virus. Either way, it's your body's quick way to clean house.

Why do we sweat?

Sweating is the body's way of cooling itself off. Whether you're stressing over a big test or running around at soccer practice, your sweat helps cool (and sometimes calm) you down. Sweat comes from a few million sweat glands in the skin.

WHY IS SWEAT SALTY?

When you sweat, your body releases salt into the sweat ducts. This draws water up to the skin's surface. Most of the salt goes back into your body, but some of it is carried to your skin, where the extra salt mixes with the watery sweat.

Everyone has millions of sweat glands.

WHY DO SOME PEOPLE SWEAT MORE THAN OTHERS?

People are just built differently. But some people who sweat a lot may have a condition called hyperhidrosis (hi-per-hi-DROH-sis). Some diseases or health conditions might also cause excessive sweating.

Why does sweat stink?

The smell of sweat comes from bacteria that live on your skin. These tiny creatures mix with sweat as it comes out of your body and cause the foul odor. Remember to wash up after you get hot and sweaty— or other people will have to remind you!

What is
hay fever?

People who suffer from *rhinitis*—commonly called hay fever—are allergic to pollen and other particles in the air. Symptoms include itchy, watery eyes, a stuffed nose, or a drippy throat. Dust mites, animal dander, mold spores, and fabric fibers can also cause hay fever. Between 10 and 30% of Americans suffer from hay fever. More than 10,000 U.S. children miss school each day because of hay fever.

WHY ARE SOME PEOPLE ALLERGIC TO CERTAIN FOODS?

Allergic reactions happen because the body's immune system, which protects the body from infections, identifies a food as something dangerous. The immune system releases chemicals that cause the symptoms of an allergic reaction. Food allergies can be very serious. In fact, more than 3 million Americans are allergic to peanuts. Millions more are allergic to fish, shellfish, dairy, and other foods.

Ah-choo!
When allergies make you sneeze, cover it up! You're still spreading germs.

Why does a flu shot work?

Influenza—commonly called "the flu"—is caused by viruses that infect the lungs and the respiratory system. Peak flu season usually occurs in January and February. The flu can spread through sneezes and coughs. A flu shot gives you a small amount of the virus that has been made harmless. Your body can practice fighting off the virus in the vaccine so that it is ready to protect you if you come across an infected person. Still, experts say the best way to keep germs away is to wash your hands.

WHY DO WE PUT ANTISEPTIC ON CUTS?

Your skin is your largest organ, and it stops a lot of bad stuff from getting into your body. When you get a cut, however, the skin's protection is broken. Germs and dirt can enter through the cut and cause infection or illness. Antiseptic is medicine that can kill bacteria before they cause trouble. Doctors will clean a cut and apply antiseptic before covering a wound with a bandage.

Why can **broken bones fix themselves?**

When a bone breaks, your body makes lots of new cells that rebuild the bone and help it heal. Bad breaks often need help from a doctor to set the bone straight, and sometimes pins and braces are also necessary. But when it comes to typical healing, the body can often help itself.

WHY DO DOCTORS USE A TOURNIQUET?

If a person cuts or damages a major blood vessel or artery, the bleeding needs to be stopped . . . fast. A tourniquet is a tightly wrapped bandage, usually made of thick cloth. It can safely stop most of the blood flow so the injured person won't bleed to death.

Why do **cuts heal?**

When you have a cut, new skin slowly builds up at the edges before covering the area entirely. Sometimes a hard scab will form over the cut, while underneath new skin is safely growing. If you eat well, your body will have the ingredients to heal better, and more quickly.

Why do we sleep ?

Sleep is important for a variety of reasons, yet scientists don't really agree on why. One theory suggests that sleep allows the brain to review all the bits of information we gather while awake. Another theory says brains need sleep to help bodies flush out waste. Still another says sleep lets people build up energy. Since sleep is critical in helping the brain and body recover and rest, doctors say kids between the ages of 6 and 13 need 9 to 11 hours of sleep each night. How do you measure up?

Why do we dream?

As with sleep, scientists don't really agree on just one reason why we dream. Some researchers say dreaming is important to our mental and physical health. Some doctors say dreams may be a reflection of a person's waking thoughts and wants.

Doctors say school-age kids should sleep 3,650 hours a year!

WHY DO WE SOMETIMES NEED NAPS?

According to the National Sleep Foundation, humans are actually unusual among mammals in that we don't nap every day. For humans who do nap, the benefits include having more energy and alertness and reducing stress.

Why is **my nose** like a shark?

Your nose isn't made only of bone. It's also made of a flexible material called cartilage. Cartilage is thin, but very strong. You also have cartilage inside your throat and in parts of your inner ear. What else is made of cartilage? A shark's skeleton! Sharks have no bones at all.

WHY DO WE HAVE FINGERNAILS?

Fingernails are handy. They help us perform a variety of tasks including scratching a bite, peeling fruit, undoing a knot, and opening a package of string cheese. Most mammals have claws or hooves of some sort. On the other hand, humans and other primates have fingernails, which are like flat claws.

Why do I get **goose bumps?**

In Spanish, *piel de gallina* means "hen skin."

Let's say you're watching a scary movie. Just before the zombie jumps out of the closet, you get goose bumps on your arms. Goose bumps, or chicken skin, are caused by immediate changes in your skin when you are cold or scared. The small muscles that are attached to the tiny hairs in your skin get tighter, or contract. This motion pulls your hair upright, causing goose bumps.

Why are people ticklish?

When someone tickles you, they aren't just fooling around. They're stimulating delicate nerve endings just under the skin. Some parts of your body are more ticklish than others. Feet are especially sensitive to tickling because feet have large nerve endings.

WHY DO I LAUGH?

Scientists don't know everything about laughter, but they do know one thing: it's caused by more than funny things. Some think laughing is another way for people to communicate that things are good and to make others happy. Laughter can be contagious. When someone next to you cracks up, you often want to laugh, too.

AROUND THE WORLD

Why is the center of Moscow called Red Square?

Page 92

Why is **London Bridge in Arizona?**

As the nursery rhyme says: "London Bridge is falling down, falling down, falling down . . ." In 1962, that was literally the case. The bridge, which spanned the Thames River in London, England, had been rebuilt several times and this version, built in 1831, was sinking under its own weight into the clay of the river. In 1968, businessman Robert McCulloch bought the bridge for $2.4 million and moved it, brick-by-brick, from England to Lake Havasu City, Arizona. By 1971, London Bridge was once again open—this time in the U.S.

The famed London Bridge was rebuilt in Arizona.

WHY IS THE CN TOWER SO HIGH AND MIGHTY?

At 1,815 feet (553 m), Toronto's CN Tower was the tallest tower in the world when it opened in 1976. It only held that title until 2010, but it's still the highest freestanding structure in the western hemisphere. Not only is it a towering titan, but it also acts as a communications hub for central Canada. The tower broadcasts about 30 TV stations, countless radio signals, and lots of cell phone calls.

WHY IS THE TOWER OF PISA LEANING?

Though Italy's most famous tower took 226 years to build, starting in 1173, the problems started in its first five years. The foundation of the 185-foot-tall (56.4-m) marble tower is a very shallow 10 feet (3.05 m) deep. Even worse, the tower is built on clay instead of bedrock. Unsurprisingly, the 14,500-ton (13,154-mt) structure tilted by the time the third floor was built in 1178. Repairs have been made consistently over 800 years, using cables, poles, and 800-ton (725 mt) weights. After 11 years of repairs, engineers re-opened the tower in 2001.

Why is the Chunnel a triumph of engineering?

ENGLAND

London

English Channel

Channel Tunnel

FRANCE

Paris

The dream of connecting Great Britain and Europe by land has been around for centuries. In 1990, crews dug tunnels under the English Channel from both England and France. The plan was to meet in the middle and complete a single tunnel. The dig called for high-tech machines, extremely careful measuring, and new tunneling techniques. It worked! Four years later, the first trains started running through the 31-mile (49.8-km) Channel Tunnel, or Chunnel.

WHY DOES THE GOLDEN GATE BRIDGE SWAY IN THE WIND?

California's Golden Gate Bridge, which spans the entry to San Francisco Bay from the Pacific Ocean, can swing sideways up to 27 feet (8.23 m). The builder, Joseph Strauss, intentionally designed the 4,200-foot (1,280-m) center span of the bridge to sway in strong ocean winds, to prevent it collapsing from the pressure.

It took four years to build the Golden Gate Bridge!

Why did France give the Statue of Liberty to the U.S.?

The statue's full name is Liberty Enlightening the World. France gave it to the people of the United States as a sign of the friendship forged between the two countries during the American Revolution (1775–1783). It was presented to honor the 100th anniversary of American independence. The world's tallest woman (151 feet/46-m) was shipped to New York, assembled, and dedicated on October 28, 1886. Lady Liberty has become a universal symbol of freedom and democracy.

WHY IS THE STATUE OF LIBERTY GREEN?

The outer layer of the Statue of Liberty, which stands in New York Harbor, is made of copper. That metal changes when exposed to water and wind. This chemical reaction causes the copper's color to go from gold/bronze to light green.

Why is the Statue of Liberty holding a torch?

French sculptor Frederic-Auguste Bartholdi designed the statue with a torch raised high in her right hand. The torch stands for enlightenment and hope for the world. The book in her other hand says July 4, 1776, in

WHY IS MURUDESHWAR AN IMPORTANT HINDU SITE?

This 123-foot (37-m) statue of Lord Shiva is in Murudeshwar, on the west coast of India. The influence of the Hindu religion is everywhere in India. Shiva, along with Brahma and Vishnu, is one of the three principal Hindu gods.

Why do Communist statues salute each other in Budapest, Hungary?

From the end of World War II, in 1945, until 1989, Hungary was controlled by the Soviet Union. When that communist country broke apart, the Hungarians were stuck with a bunch of unwanted statues of their former leaders. To help Hungarians put those difficult times in perspective, they moved the statues to an open-air museum called Memento Park, arranging the once-powerful leaders to harmlessly command and salute only each other.

Why was a huge statue built over Rio de Janeiro, Brazil?

With his arms outstretched, a 98-foot (30-m) tall statue of Jesus stands guard on a mountaintop towering over the large city of Rio. It was built in 1931 to provide a symbol of faith to the people of this heavily Catholic country. A popular tourist attraction, the statue is made of concrete covered with soapstone.

Why is this **mosque in Timbuktu unique?**

First built more than 600 years ago, the Djingareyber mosque in Mali is the world's largest building made of mud. Some descendants of the original builders still work to maintain the ancient building, which remains in daily use.

WHY DOES SOUTH AFRICA HAVE THREE CAPITAL CITIES?

South Africans disagreed originally on where to put a capital city, so they chose a different capital city for each of their three branches of government. The president and administration are in Pretoria; the judicial capital is in Johannesberg; and the parliamentary legislature is in Cape Town.

Why is **climbing Mt. Kilimanjaro so popular?**

Mt. Kilimanjaro in Tanzania is Africa's tallest peak, topping out at 19,341 feet (5,895 m). Most mountains of such heights are very difficult and dangerous to climb. Kilimanjaro's gentle slopes, however, make it possible for many people to reach the top. More than 40,000 people make the long walk each year. The youngest hiker to reach the top was only six years old!

WHY DID THE EGYPTIANS MUMMIFY THE DEAD?

Ancient Egyptians believed that the dead should look as they did when they were alive. Bodies were treated with special chemicals that helped to stop decay. To help the bodies retain their shape, they were tightly wrapped in linen strips. They were often decorated with beads and buried with their belongings.

Why did the ancient Egyptians **build the Great Pyramid?**

The Great Pyramid of Giza is probably the grandest ancient building in the world. Built from more than 2 million limestone blocks ranging in weight from 2.5 tons (2,268 kg) to 15 tons (13.6 mt) each, the 4,500-year-old pyramid was built as a tomb for King Khufu. Inside the pyramids and other tombs, the ancient Egyptians placed gold, sculptures, furniture, and other treasure that the king might need in the afterlife. The pyramid shape was considered sacred.

HOW DID ANCIENT EGYPTIANS MUMMIFY THE DEAD?

Internal organs—including the lungs, stomach, and intestines—were removed through a hole in the body. The brain was removed through the nose. Then, scientists believe, the priests used a special salt to dry out the body. They packed the skull with salt and plaster, replacing the eyes with artificial ones. Organs were put into jars, and the body was wrapped in linen and made ready for the afterlife.

The Great Sphinx of Giza is half human, half lion, and stands 65 feet (19.8 m) high.

Why are the Galapagos Islands unique?

The remote Galapagos Islands, off the coast of Ecuador, are home to unique species of plant and animal life, including tortoises, seals, penguins, and blue-footed boobies, that are not found anywhere else on Earth. So incredible are its natural treasures that they inspired Charles Darwin's theory of evolution. Certain areas are open to tour groups, who are led by guides to make sure the area is not disturbed.

WHY ISN'T EVEREST THE WORLD'S TALLEST MOUNTAIN?

Though only 13,796 feet (4,205 m) above sea level, Mauna Kea, on the Island of Hawaii, stands 33,000 feet (10,058m) high when measured from its base far under the Pacific Ocean. That makes it "taller" than Mt. Everest in Nepal, which stands 29,035 feet (8,848 m) from base to tip.

Why are these statues on Easter Island?

Easter Island is one of the world's most isolated spots. It is about 2,300 miles (3,701 km) west of mainland Chile, in the South Pacific. Ancient statues, called *moais* (moh-eyes), are scattered across the island. Each is carved from a single stone. Some are more than 30 feet (9.1 m) tall.

Why are there so many cowboys in Argentina?

The wide grasslands of central Argentina, known as the *pampas*, are perfect for raising cattle—wide and flat with huge areas of grass. Cowboys called *gauchos* work the huge herds that live in Argentina. The beef of these free-range cattle is considered by many to be the world's most delicious.

Which continent is on top of the world —North America or South America?

Some South American mapmakers defy tradition with maps and globes that feature Antarctica, Africa, and South America pointing upward, not down. Our common view of the world map comes from long-ago Europeans who, naturally, saw their countries on top. But in reality, we live on a globe spinning through space. There's no right answer!

Antártida

Australia

América del Sur

África

Asia   Europa   Norteamérica

WHY DO PEOPLE IN BRAZIL SPEAK PORTUGUESE?

For 300 years, beginning in 1500, Brazil was a colony of Portugal. When Brazil gained its independence in 1822, the language remained. Most of the rest South America had been controlled by Spain, which is why many South Americans speak Spanish today.

87

Why do so many people live near the Ganges River?

The Ganges River (called *Ganga* in Hindi) runs from the Himalaya mountains to the Indian Ocean. About 400 million people—almost a third of India's population, and a little more than 5% of the world's population—depend on this 1,569-mile (2,525-km) river for survival. It irrigates land and nourishes animals. Also, being a holy river to Hindus, it serves as a funeral site for thousands of people every day.

WHY DO COWS WALK FREELY THROUGH INDIA?

Thanks to their life-giving milk, cows are honored as a symbol of life in the Hindu religion. This is why devout Hindus will not eat beef, and many feel they shouldn't even disturb or bother cows who wander through the streets. When a cow lies down in traffic, it's the drivers who give way.

Why is this Turkish mosque's story much like Istanbul itself?

The massive Hagia Sophia in Istanbul mirrors the history of its Turkish home. The building began its life in 532 as a vast Catholic church called Sancta Sophia, a symbol of the power of the Byzantine Empire. In 1453, the empire fell to an Ottoman sultan, who converted the building into a mosque. In 1934, the government of Turkey, which has no official religion, made it a museum.

Why is **Mount Fuji a symbol for Japan?**

Mount Fuji is Japan's tallest mountain. The 12,388-foot (3,773-m) high volcano, which last erupted in 1707, is also a national park. It's surrounded by five lakes. In the summer, thousands climb to the top. The hike takes three to eight hours.

Why are many Japanese trains so fast?

First built in the 1960s, the "bullet trains," known in Japanese as *Shinkansen*, can reach speeds of 200 miles (320 km) per hour. The trains are sleek and aerodynamic, like missiles, shaped to cut through the wind. Long, straight tracks are used, avoiding curves which would reduce the train's speed. Having fewer stops than most trains also allows the *Shinkansen* to reach full speed and keep up the momentum.

WHY WAS THE ANGKOR WAT TEMPLE BUILT?

Angkor Wat, in Cambodia, is one of the most famous sites in the world. The temple complex at the center of an ancient city was built to honor the Hindu religion more than 800 years ago and later became a Buddhist temple. Its builders used more than 5 million stone blocks, each weighing up to 3,000 pounds (1,360 kg).

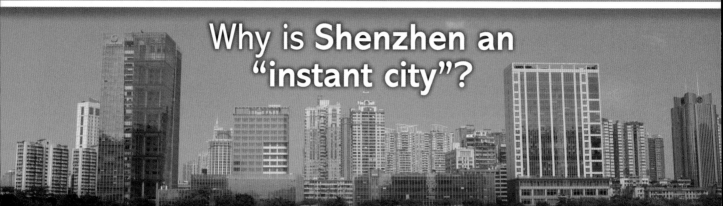

Why is Shenzhen an "instant city"?

Not long ago, Shenzhen was a small fishing village about 10 miles (17 km) from giant Hong Kong. China wanted a much larger city in the region to house Hong Kong's workers. So the central government created an "instant city." In 1980, only 30,000 people lived in Shenzhen. In 1992, 3 million called it home. Today, more than 10 million people live in Shenzhen, and the city is still growing.

Why did the Chinese build

the Great Wall?

The Great Wall of China is actually a series of separate walls that were built over a period of 2000 years, beginning in the 7th Century B.C. The walls take advantage of high peaks, cliffs, and rivers to create a barrier against invading armies. An archeological survey in 2012 found that the Great Wall of China, with all of its branches and side walls, is 13,748 miles (21,196 km) long.

WHY ARE PORCELAIN DISHES CALLED "CHINA"?

In 618 B.C, the Chinese discovered how to make dishes stronger by adding the minerals feldspar and kaolin to clay, creating porcelain. European explorers, including Marco Polo, amazed the folks back home with the beautiful dishes they called China, in honor of the place where they were created.

Why is an area in Beijing, China, called the Forbidden City?

Located in the middle of Beijing, the capital of China, the Forbidden City was once the imperial palace of Ming and Qing Dynasty rulers. The city, built between 1406 and 1420, served as the emperor's home and the political and ceremonial center of the country for more than 500 years. The area's 900-plus buildings were called the Forbidden City because only China's royal family could enter without special permission. Today, the area is a popular tourist spot.

The Forbidden City isn't forbidden anymore!

WHY ARE THOUSANDS OF CLAY SOLDIERS BURIED IN XI'AN, CHINA?

The Chinese emperor Qin Shi Huang Di (born 259 B.C.) wanted a magnificent tomb. He got it, though it took several years to build. To protect him in the afterlife, the emperor ordered a vast guardian army of thousands of life-sized soldiers made of a clay called terra cotta. Horses, chariots, and bronze weapons were also buried with him when he died in 210 B.C. This giant city of the dead wasn't uncovered again until 1974.

WHY DO THE NAMES OF MANY COUNTRIES IN CENTRAL ASIA END IN "-STAN"?

Seven Central Asian countries have a name ending in "-stan": Afghanistan, Kazakhstan, Kyrgyzstan, Pakistan, Tajikistan, Turkmenistan, and Uzbekistan. The suffix "-stan" is ancient Persian for "land" or "country." So, for example, Afghanistan is Land of the Afghans.

Why are Russian church domes shaped like onions?

Russian Orthodox churches have featured these domes for more than 1,000 years. Some historians think the design was influenced by Russia's Islamic neighbors. Others say they're meant to look like burning candles. Regardless, they're practical: heavy Russian snow slides off easily.

Why is the center of Moscow called Red Square?

Moscow's central square has existed since at least the 15th century. The area was once called Krasnyi, which originally meant "beautiful" but later became the word for the color red. It's true that red was also the color of the Communist Party that ruled the Soviet Union from 1917 to 1989, but Red Square's name came centuries before that.

Why does the Aboriginal musical instrument called a didgeridoo depend on termites?

Aborigines, the people who first settled in Australia at least 40,000 years ago, have been playing this tubular instrument for centuries. They make low, eerie sounds by blowing into the tubes or making a buzzing sound that echoes. Why are insects involved? The best didgeridoos are made from eucalyptus trees that have been hollowed out by termites. The termites' tunnel patterns create a unique sound for each instrument.

WHY IS AUSTRALIA CALLED "THE LAND DOWN UNDER"?

When Europeans started going south to Australia, they felt it was at the bottom of the world. Australia was below the Equator, and "down under" just about everything on the European world map. Of course, if they'd used the map on page 87, the nickname would be "the land up over."

Why do Maori people use face paint and tattoos?

Maori people were the first to live in New Zealand. Their traditions are still celebrated today. This Maori man has *moko*, or tattoos, on his face. Such markings identify a person's tribe and their rank or position in the tribe.

93

HISTORY

Why were computer users afraid of January 1, 2000?

Page 124

Why were the ancient Romans so powerful?

Ancient Rome was once the mightiest civilization on the planet. From about 31 B.C. to 476 A.D., Rome controlled a large portion of the world, including much of Europe, a chunk of North Africa, and the western Middle East. Rome owed its power to its organizational skill, the brilliance of its generals, and the might of its army. It was also ahead of the curve with its technology and ideas, including roads, irrigation, science, and education.

What were Roman families like?

The average Roman family consisted of two parents and five or six kids. Wealthy Roman families sent their children to school, while those with less money did not. In most households, boys and girls worked long hours in the fields. Many families owned slaves who worked in homes and fields. They were generally bought or taken from conquered lands.

Julius Caesar created a "newspaper" to let everyone know what Rome's leaders were doing.

WHO WAS JULIUS CAESAR?

Julius Caesar was a Roman politician and general who helped transform Rome into the center of a great empire. He dominated Roman society and was proclaimed "dictator in perpetuity," meaning forever. A group of Roman senators, led by Marcus Junius Brutus, killed Caesar in 44 B.C. hoping to restore the Roman republic.

What destroyed the ancient city of Pompeii?

On August 24, 79 A.D., an eerie darkness covered parts of southern Italy as Vesuvius, a 4,200-foot-high (1,280 m) volcano, blew its top. Boiling mud and lava poured down the side of the mountain, burning everything in its path. Thousands in the nearby cities of Pompeii and Herculaneum raced to the sea to escape fiery death. Thousands more could not outrun the ash and lava. The city was destroyed.

WHY ARE SOME PEOPLE STILL AFRAID OF VESUVIUS?

Since 79 A.D., Mount Vesuvius has erupted about 35 times with tremendous force, and many people fear it will blow again. The next eruption could cause major damage. About 600,000 people live in 18 towns in the so-called *zona rossa*, or red zone, close to Vesuvius. Scientists say during the first 15 minutes of an eruption, anything within a 4 mile (6.44 km) radius could be destroyed, including many towns in the red zone.

WHY IS THE ANCIENT CITY OF POMPEII SO WELL PRESERVED?

When Vesuvius finished spitting lava and ash on that awful day in 79 A.D., the eruption had blanketed Pompeii and other cities under a layer of ash and mud, preserving the city forever. The bodies of victims left their shapes in the volcanic ash. Scientists used the volcanic molds to create concrete casts of many who had been caught in the eruption.

Why did the Maya build pyramids?

The Maya were native people of Mexico and Central America, whose civilization flourished from about 300 A.D. to 900 A.D. They built large cities and traded with people of other cultures. They also built pyramids, mostly for religious purposes. Some pyramids had stairs so people could climb to the top and hold sacrificial rituals. The Maya built the pyramids taller than the surrounding jungle so people could use them as landmarks. The Maya also used some pyramids as tombs for important government officials.

Some Maya pyramids are as tall as a 20-story building.

WHY WAS ONE MAYA BALL GAME DEADLY SERIOUS?

Basketball, baseball, and soccer are popular ball games for a reason: they're fun. In ancient Mayan society, the ball game Pok-ta-Pok wasn't as fun. The goal of the game was to pass a rubber ball and get it through a ring without using hands. The winners were treated as heroes and given a feast. The losers were put to death.

WHY DID THE MAYA CIVILIZATION DISAPPEAR?

For 1,200 years, Maya society dominated life in Mexico and Central America. Maya cities were crammed with people. Then the Maya civilization disappeared. NASA scientists say drought and deforestation may have caused the Maya civilization to collapse. To survive in hard times, they cut down the jungle to grow corn to feed their ever-growing population. They also cut trees for firewood and for building homes. The deforestation destroyed their land.

Why were bison vital to Plains Indians?

These large, shaggy mammals were an important resource for Native Americans. Plains Indians, including the Sioux, Cheyenne, and Comanche tribes, ate the bison's meat; used its hide for clothing and tipi covers; shaped its bones, hooves, and horns for tools and ceremonial objects; and even used its dung for fuel. The bison lived in herds of thousands of animals, on what is now the western prairie of the United States.

WHY WERE NATIVE AMERICANS CALLED INDIANS?

Some mistakes stick around. 15th and 16th century Europeans who were sailing to India had no idea that uncharted North America would to get in the way (see page 104). They believed they had landed in India. The word *Indian* came to mean anyone who was native to this "New World." Only recently, more accurate terms such as *Native Americans* began to be used. Another term—First Nations people—is used primarily in Canada.

Why could Inuit people walk from Asia to North America?

Until about 13,000 years ago, Asia and North America were connected across the Bering Sea near the Arctic by a wide strip of land that is now underwater. Until the land bridge disappeared, the Asian people who became today's Inuit walked to what is now Alaska, and some of their descendants continued all the way to the southern tip of South America.

Why is the *Vasa* Sweden's most famous ship?

The wooden warship *Vasa* set sail from Sweden in 1628, but was too top-heavy and sank just offshore on its first voyage. In 1956, 328 years later, it was rediscovered and in 1961, it was brought to the surface in amazing condition. The *Vasa* serves as a vital link to Sweden's long maritime tradition. The ship was restored and is now the centerpiece of a museum in Stockholm.

WHY DID THE VIKINGS LEAVE HOME?

Historians note several reasons why Viking people from Scandinavia sailed to other parts of Europe and even North America. The mighty Vikings sought new places to trade and new places to plunder. Their population was also growing, creating the need for more farm land. Whatever the reasons, the far-ranging Vikings spread their culture wherever they went. For instance, our Wednesday, Thursday, and Friday are named for the Norse gods Odin, Thor, and Freitag.

Did Vikings really have horns on their helmets?

Although the Minnesota Vikings have painted horns on their football helmets, the real Vikings of Scandinavia did not wear horned helmets. It's true that many ancient cultures wore horned helmets for ceremonies. However, the helmets fell out of fashion by the time of the Vikings. If you see a painting of Vikings with horns on their helmets, you know the artist made a mistake.

Why did the Crusades begin?

Led by kings and knights, Christian warriors marched from Europe into the Middle East in an attempt to capture the "Holy Land" near Jerusalem from Muslim rulers. Those invasions were known as the Crusades. The First Crusade began in 1096, when a highly-trained force, including 4,000 knights on horseback and 25,000 foot soldiers, moved east. There were a total of eight crusades. The last one started in 1270.

WHY WERE KNIGHTS IMPORTANT IN MEDIEVAL EUROPE?

During Europe's Middle Ages (between the 5th and 16th centuries), kings ruled over serfs and peasants. Armed warriors, known as knights, were the law enforcement division, helping kings, other royalty, and even wealthy landlords protect their land and promote their interests. Knights often received land in return for their successes in battle and for their loyalty.

WHY DID PEOPLE BUILD CASTLES?

During the first part of the Middle Ages, common people generally built homes out of straw, mud, and stone. But by about 1000 A.D., wealthy Europeans were erecting impressive churches and castles out of giant stones. Thick stone walls offered royalty protection from attacking armies and angry, frustrated peasants. Towers and spires, steeply-pitched roofs, and magnificent archways impressed the commoners and awed visitors.

High stone walls served as home security systems in the Middle Ages.

Why was the Hundred Years War bad news for Britain?

In 1337, a small piece of land in southwestern France, called Aquitaine, technically belonged to Britain. France wanted its land back, and the two nations fought for 116 years. Finally, in 1453, English troops were forced out of France for good.

Longbows were highly accurate weapons.

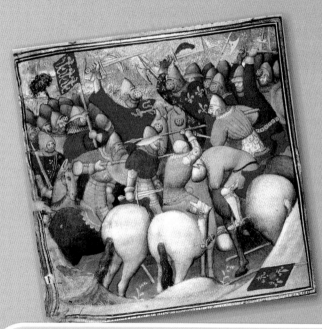

WHY WAS THE LONGBOW A MILITARY GAME CHANGER?

Beginning in the early 1300s, British troops used the longbow to attack their enemies from a great distance. The powerful bows could shoot arrows hundreds of yards (or meters). By hitting enemies before they could launch their own attacks, English armies won many important battles.

WHY WAS THE MAGNA CARTA SO IMPORTANT?

Signed by England's King John in 1215, the Magna Carta contained the first laws that allowed its citizens the right to approve the rules that governed them. It also forced the king to follow laws, too. It was an important step toward modern European democracy.

Why is the printing press one of the **most important inventions of all time?**

It's very possible that the printing press is the most significant invention in modern history—even greater than the smart phone! Prior to the mid-1400s, book production was a long, hard, and expensive process. Only a few books existed, and only rich people could afford them. That all changed when Johannes Gutenberg, a German inventor, invented the printing press in 1440. The press made it easier to print books, meaning more people could read—and learn.

Before he was a printer, Johannes Gutenberg was a goldsmith.

WHY WAS THE GUTENBERG BIBLE THE FIRST MODERN BOOK?

The first book to roll off Gutenberg's modern printing press was a Bible, in 1455. The type was easier to read than handwriting. Because of the mechanical press and mass-produced, moveable metal type, the books could be reproduced much more quickly and easily than handmade books. No one knows how many Gutenberg Bibles were printed, but historians estimate at least 180. Only 49 are known to survive today.

Why did **telescopes change our understanding of Earth?**

Before telescopes were invented in the Netherlands in the 1500s, humans could only use their eyes to see the moon and stars. Telescopes let humans see the heavens more accurately. Scientists quickly discovered Earth was not, in fact, the center of the universe, or even the Solar System, as was widely believed. By showing that our planet was a smaller part of a greater system, telescopes helped bring us back down to Earth.

Why did Christopher Columbus sail to America?

It wasn't on purpose. When Columbus sailed west across the Atlantic from Spain in 1492, he was looking for a fast route to Asia. No one in Europe knew a New World existed. At the time, European ships traveled east around the tip of Africa to get to Asia. Columbus first landed in the Caribbean believing he was in India, but he never actually set foot in North America.

WHY DID EUROPEAN EXPLORERS CAUSE PROBLEMS IN THE NEW WORLD?

Columbus opened the door for Europeans to come westward. When the Europeans saw the New World, they took treasures from the ground and, worse, they exploited and killed the natives. Invaders made slaves of the people they found, took their land, and brought guns, weeds, rats, and especially diseases, all of which were bad news for natives.

WHY WAS CHRISTOPHER COLUMBUS ARRESTED?

Christopher Columbus first landed on the Caribbean island of Hispaniola, where he left some of his crew to set up a colony. When he returned in 1493, he found the colony in chaos and tried to restore order. Many colonists went back to Spain and complained about how Columbus ran the colony. A royal governor then came to America and arrested Columbus. When Columbus returned to Spain, the king and queen spared him from prison.

WHY DID THE BRITISH SEND ITS PRISONERS TO AUSTRALIA?

In the late 1700s, Britain's prisons were becoming dangerous and overcrowded so it sent convicts to its American colonies. That option vanished after the Americans won their independence in 1783. Britain's next move was to send its prisoners on a far longer journey to Australia, which had been added to the British empire in 1770.

Why did the Spanish want American colonies?

With its powerful army and ocean-going ships, Spain saw the New World as a place from which they could take many riches and plant their colonial flag. In Central and South America, the Spanish conquered the native peoples and stole their natural resources. They also wanted to spread their Catholic religion in their new colonies.

Why did the Dutch fight the Boer Wars in South Africa?

In the early 1800s, England had taken most of South Africa's Cape Colony from the Dutch. By the middle of the century, some Dutch settlers, known as Boers (farmers), had settled their own land away from the colony, farther inland. By the late 1800s, England wanted those lands as colonies, too. The battles went on for years, but England eventually won in 1902. South Africa finally became independent of Great Britain in 1961.

Why did the Pilgrims want to escape England?

Many of the Pilgrims were Puritans from the English Separatist church. They were being persecuted by the dominant Church of England. Looking for a place to worship freely, the Puritans set their sights on the New World, arriving in Plymouth, Massachusetts, in 1620.

WHY DID PENNSYLVANIA GET ITS NAME?

William Penn was a British gentleman of the Quaker religion. England didn't offer him freedom of religion. In 1670, Penn got land in the New World from King Charles II, who owed Penn's father money. In 1682, Penn arrived at his new, tree-covered land. *Silva* is Latin for forest, which makes the actual name Penn's Forest.

Why did the **first colony** at Roanoke disappear?

A group of English colonists landed there in 1587. Four years later, another group arrived, but could find no trace of the original settlers. After studying area trees, scientists now believe that a drought had led to starvation. A similar drought affected a colony in Jamestown several years later.

Why did the American Revolution begin in Massachusetts?

When the expensive French and Indian War ended in 1763, England wanted its American colonies to pay war costs. The British parliament passed laws requiring American colonists to pay new taxes. The colonists did not receive the new tax laws well—not because their tax burden was high, but because they were not represented in Parliament. So they protested, particularly around the wealthy port city of Boston, Massachusetts. The king sent governors and red-coated soldiers to enforce laws and collect money. By 1775, frustration and anger boiled over, soldiers openly clashed with colonists, and Massachusetts was declared to be in rebellion. War had begun.

WHY DID PAUL REVERE TAKE HIS FAMOUS MIDNIGHT RIDE?

With revolution brewing, American colonists had stockpiled gunpowder and weapons in Concord, Massachusetts. Two patriots, Sam Adams and John Hancock, were discovered by the British to be hiding in nearby Lexington. On April 18, 1775, British troops advanced on the area to capture what (and who) they could. Alerted by spies and a two-lantern early warning system, Paul Revere and William Dawes rode 20 miles from Boston to warn the Patriots. They were joined on the way by Samuel Prescott. The next day, the war's first battles were fought at Lexington and Concord.

WHY WAS THE DECLARATION OF INDEPENDENCE WRITTEN?

By mid-1776, after more than a year of battles, the patriots' Continental Congress agreed to unite the colonies and dissolve bonds with England. It drafted a formal document explaining the many reasons the colonies were seeking independence, and declaring that all men had a right to "life, liberty, and the pursuit of happiness." The Declaration served to rally colonial troops and justify the war to other countries.

WHY IS WASHINGTON, D.C., AMERICA'S CAPITAL?

In the earliest days of the United States, the capital moved around. The first U.S. capital was in New York City, from 1785 to 1790. Then, the capital moved to Philadelphia. Meanwhile, members of Congress from the North and South argued over where the nation's permanent home should be. After negotiations, lawmakers took land from Maryland and Virginia on the banks of the Potomac River to create a diamond-shaped capital.

The capital was named for the first president, who died in 1796, and it was first occupied in 1800. The term District of Columbia separates it from ownership by any state.

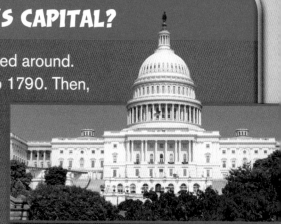

Why is the White House called the White House?

When it was first used in 1800, the building was known as the President's House. In 1811, it was painted white all over, but kept its original name (though some called it the Executive Mansion). In 1901, President Theodore Roosevelt officially dubbed the mansion the White House, when he had the name printed on his stationery.

Why were the White House and U.S. Capitol built by slaves?

The brand-new city of Washington, D.C., was built from farmland and swamps. However, the land was still part of the South in the late 1700s and early 1800s, where slavery was legal. Many of the builders brought their own personal slaves with them to work on the job. They also contracted with plantation owners around the city to use their slaves, because slaves aren't paid labor.

John Adams was the first president to live in the White House.

Why did pirates inspire the creation of the U.S. Navy?

After the Revolutionary War, the new American nation broke up its navy. Soon after, pirates in North Africa attacked American merchant ships. Something had to be done. The U.S. government sent several warships to deal with the problem. The success of their mission led the U.S. to officially set up the U.S. Navy in 1794 in order to be ready to deal with future problems on the high seas.

Why was Andrew Jackson known as Old Hickory?

The future president was an Army officer during the War of 1812. In 1813, he and his soldiers were forced to make a long and difficult march. Instead of acting like most officers—riding a horse and eating the best food—Jackson walked with his men to encourage them to keep going. His soldiers started calling him Old Hickory after the tough hickory trees they passed on the march.

WHY DID DOLLY MADISON CARRY A PORTRAIT OF GEORGE WASHINGTON OUT OF THE WHITE HOUSE?

So it wouldn't get burned! In August 1814, Great Britain and the United States were fighting the War of 1812. On August 24, the British army was marching toward Washington, D.C. The Americans lost a battle a few miles from the capital city. With Washington, D.C., the next target, Dolly Madison, the wife of President James Madison, fled the White House, taking a full-length portrait of George Washington with her. That same evening the British burned many buildings, including the White House, but the portrait was saved.

Dolly Madison

109

The Underground Railroad was a vast network dedicated to freedom.

What was the Underground Railroad?

The Underground Railroad wasn't an actual railroad. It was a complex system that allowed as many as 100,000 slaves to escape from the South to freedom, using the language of railroads. The slaves followed routes called lines. People who helped the slaves along the lines were conductors. Houses along the way where slaves hid were stations. The slaves were called packages. Many people, black and white, risked punishment and even their lives to help slaves reach freedom.

Why did escaping slaves go to Canada?

The number of slaves escaping to freedom in the north angered many Southerners. After the U.S. Congress passed the Fugitive Slave Act in 1850, it became illegal to assist escaped slaves in Northern states. So, escaping slaves used the Underground Railroad to escape to the "promised land" of Canada.

WHY WAS HARRIET TUBMAN AN IMPORTANT CONDUCTOR ON THE UNDERGROUND RAILROAD?

Harriet Tubman was a slave who escaped from Maryland and fled North to freedom in 1849. By 1860, Tubman had helped more than 300 other slaves escape to freedom. She later became a leader in the movement to free all slaves.

Slaves were often bought and sold at public auctions.

Why did Americans buy and sell slaves?

The first slaves came to America in 1619, when a Dutch ship brought 20 enslaved Africans to the Virginia colony of Jamestown. To wealthy white owners, slaves were the cheap and dependable source of labor they needed to work their tobacco, sugar, rice, and, later, cotton plantations. They also worked in homes and businesses in the North. Unfortunately, the hard work of slaves became vital to America's growing economy. Over some 200 years, hundreds of thousands of slaves were brought to British North America, until the international slave trade was outlawed in 1808. Ultimately the slave population of the United States would reach 4 million.

Why was the Civil War fought?

As the U.S. grew, Americans disagreed over expanding slavery to new Western states. Southern lawmakers wanted to extend slavery to these territories to support their farming economy; many Northerners wanted slavery abolished everywhere. When Abraham Lincoln, who was viewed as anti-slavery by many, was elected president in 1860, a group of southern states seceded from the United States and formed the Confederate States of America. Soon after, fighting began. The bloodiest war in our nation's history raged for four years, from 1861 to 1865.

Why did the Industrial Revolution begin in Britain?

The Industrial Revolution was the era when more products were being made in factories, rather than at home. It began in Britain in the mid-1700s because the country had a stable government and a wealthy economy that made it possible for businessmen to build factories. Britain was also home to brilliant scientists, whose great inventions led to innovative new products.

Machines helped launch the Industrial Revolution.

WHY WERE MACHINES IMPORTANT TO THE INDUSTRIAL REVOLUTION?

Machines were the engines that drove the factories of the Industrial Revolution. Machines made items more quickly and cheaply. To power these machines, the new steam engine was far stronger than the old water wheel. Another new device, the carding machine, turned wool into yarn far more efficiently than the spinning wheel and handloom.

What is **Charles Darwin's** theme of **evolution**?

When Charles Darwin published his book *On the Origin of Species* in 1859, it sent shockwaves through the world. In the book, Darwin outlined his theories of natural selection and evolution. According to Darwin, plants and animals (including humans) *evolved*, or changed, over time. He said organisms inherit new characteristics that allow them to survive and reproduce—a process known as natural selection. Darwin also wrote that all living things came from a single common ancestor.

Charles Darwin first wanted to be a clergyman.

Why did Charles Darwin sail the world?

In 1831, Darwin set sail on the *HMS Beagle* as an unpaid botanist on a British scientific expedition. In South America, Darwin found fossils of animals that were extinct, but resembled modern species. In the Galapagos Islands in the Pacific Ocean, Darwin found many plants and animals of familiar species that had new characteristics. These and other observations led Darwin to his theories about how life evolved over millions of years.

Darwin spent five years aboard the *HMS Beagle*.

WHY DID FACTORY POLLUTION GIVE CERTAIN BUTTERFLIES AN ADVANTAGE?

Survival of the fittest—called natural selection—is a cornerstone of Darwin's theory of evolution. One example makes it very clear. In the early 1800s, before air-polluting factories were common, white butterflies thrived because they were hard for predators to find. However, factory soot soon darkened the English landscape, causing white butterflies to stand out. Darker butterflies were more fit to survive. By the 1850s, populations of darker butterflies had risen drastically, while the numbers of white butterflies fell.

113

Why was World War I called the "War to End All Wars"?

World War I (1914–1918) was a bloody, brutal war. New inventions such as tanks, poison gas, modern artillery, and the machine gun made killing far easier than in previous wars. Twelve years after its invention, the airplane was dropping bombs. More than 17 million people died. The war was so bloody and so destructive that many hoped it would be the last war ever—"The War to End all Wars."

Why did the United States enter World War I?

The U.S. was neutral early in the war, but by 1917, most Americans sided with the British and French, who were fighting the Germans in World War I. Americans were angry because German submarines, or U-boats, were sinking ships and threatening American trade. In 1915, the Germans sank the *RMS Lusitania*, a British ocean liner, killing 128 American passengers. The Germans stopped the U-boat attacks until 1917, when they were resumed in an all-out attempt to defeat Britain. On April 6, 1917, the U.S. Congress declared war on Germany.

I WANT YOU FOR U.S. ARMY
NEAREST RECRUITING STATION

American troops in World War I were part of the American Expeditionary Force.

WHY WERE AMERICAN SOLDIERS CALLED DOUGHBOYS?

Doughboy was slang for a U.S. soldier in World War I. Many think that during the Mexican-American War (1846–1848), dust-covered soldiers looked like unbaked dough. Some say they looked like *adobes*, the clay bricks which were commonly used to build Mexican homes. Others believe the term began in the 1840s and 1850s, when soldiers baked a dough-like mixture in their campfires.

Why was the **Great Depression so devastating?**

The 1930s were a terrible time in the United States. On October 27, 1929, the stock market crashed, sparking the Great Depression, the biggest economic disaster in U.S. history. Banks and stores closed and factories went out of business. Farmers could not pay their mortgages, and people lost their homes, jobs, and life savings. When Franklin Roosevelt became President in 1933, about one out of every four working-age Americans was out of work.

Soup kitchens were heavily relied on during the Great Depression.

WHY DID FRANKLIN ROOSEVELT USE A WHEELCHAIR?

When Franklin Roosevelt was 39 years old, he became ill with polio. The disease left him unable to walk. Although he spent the rest of his life in a wheelchair, he did not let the disease hold him back. He became governor of New York, and later, the only president of the United States to be elected four times.

1882 1982 USA 20c

Franklin D. Roosevelt

Why did the **Great Depression end?**

The Great Depression lasted about 10 years. When Franklin Roosevelt became president, he started programs to create jobs and slowly end the Depression. Roosevelt championed New Deal legislation such as Social Security and welfare relief. America cared for the economic and social well-being of its citizens by creating jobs, controlling banks, and providing money to people out of work. While the New Deal reduced unemployment and helped millions of Americans, only World War II—with the millions of factory jobs it created—truly ended the Great Depression.

Why did some Japanese pilots call themselves kamikazes?

Toward the end of World War II in the Pacific Ocean, it was becoming clear that Japan was losing. In a last-ditch effort for victory, some Japanese pilots flew their airplanes directly into Allied ships, attempting to sink them. These suicide attacks took the name *kamikaze*, which means divine wind in Japanese. The name was inspired by an event in 1281, when the mighty winds of a typhoon destroyed a fleet of Mongol (Chinese) ships on their way to invade Japan.

WHY WERE GLIDERS FLOWN AT D-DAY?

Allied forces planned a major invasion of France to fight back against German forces in World War II. To help pave the way for this D-Day assault, on June 6, 1944, troops were flown behind enemy lines in silent, engine-less gliders. They were towed through the air to the area behind transport aircraft. Gliders were better at concentrating troops close to the target than parachute drops, which tended to scatter the troops. Larger gliders could also carry heavier equipment, a big boost for lightly-armed paratroopers. And, by landing silently, glider troops were able to get a head start on the fighting.

Why did Germany start World War II?

World War I left Germany destroyed and impoverished. By the early 1930s, Adolf Hitler's Nazi Party rose to power by promising a return to greatness. Hitler convinced Germans that they were a chosen race who deserved to be united in an expanded Germany. Hitler blamed Jews for Germany's problems and began to punish and kill them. By 1938, Germany had built the most powerful army and air force in Europe. In September 1939, Germany invaded Poland. At

Why did the Japanese bomb Pearl Harbor?

By the end of 1941, Japan had begun conquering parts of China and Southeast Asia. It had invaded French Indochina beginning in the previous year. In response, the United States applied economic pressure on Japan, including cutting off oil shipments. To freely build its empire, Japan came up with a secret plan to destroy the U.S. Navy fleet based at Pearl Harbor, Hawaii. The attack occurred on December 7, 1941. The next day, the United States declared war on Japan.

More than 2,000 people died at Pearl Harbor.

WHY DID THE U.S. DROP ATOMIC BOMBS ON JAPAN?

World War II ended in Europe on May 8, 1945. The U.S. and its allies could then focus on winning the war against Japan. President Harry Truman ordered two atomic bombs to be dropped on the island nation to force the Japanese to surrender. The first bomb exploded over Hiroshima on August 6, 1945. Three days later, another atomic bomb exploded at Nagasaki. As many as 225,000 civilians were killed or wounded in the first and only wartime use of nuclear weapons, leading to Japan's surrender on August 15, 1945.

WHY DO KIDS SEND PAPER CRANES TO JAPAN?

Each year, kids from around the world send paper cranes as a sign of peace to the Children's Monument in Hiroshima's Peace Park. The cranes were inspired by the story of Sadako Sasaki, who was two when the bomb was dropped on Hiroshima. The radiation made her sick and she died of leukemia in 1955. While in the hospital, she began folding cranes, believing that if she folded 1,000 she would be granted one wish. She only folded 644 before her death, but her friends folded the other 356 for her.

117

What was the Cold War?

For almost 50 years following World War II, the U.S. and the U.S.S.R. were bitter enemies. That period is known as the Cold War, because the two enemies never fought with weapons. It was a war of ideas and competition between two systems of government: Democracy versus Communism. The two nations made military treaties with several other nations. Each side tried to gain superiority in space, sports, and nuclear weapons. The Cold War ended with the fall of the Soviet Union in 1991.

The race to build nuclear weapons played a big part in the Cold War.

What was the Iron Curtain?

Throughout the Cold War, the term Iron Curtain was used by democratic countries to describe the line that separated Eastern and Western Europe. This curtain symbolized a physical as well as political boundary between two ways of life. This famous phrase was coined in 1946 by England's then-former prime minister, Winston Churchill, who said an "iron curtain" had descended across Europe. On one side of that curtain, said Churchill, the Soviet Union ruled its new communist allies with an iron fist.

WHAT WAS THE BERLIN WALL?

After World War II, the Berlin Wall literally divided West Berlin and East Berlin during the Cold War. The Soviet Union and its allies controlled East Germany and East Berlin. The United States and its allies controlled West Germany and West Berlin. On August 13, 1961, the East German government built a wall across the city to stop those living in East Berlin from escaping to the West. The wall stayed up for 28 years, until the Soviet empire began to collapse and the Wall came down.

In the years after World War II, a great fear arose in the U.S. that the Soviet Union would attack with nuclear weapons. The U.S. government, hoping to prepare people for this deadly possibility, devised the duck-and-cover drill. Bells would ring at school to signal an air raid drill. Students were told to get under their desks to protect themselves from falling debris in the event of an attack. Fortunately, no such attack ever came.

Why were American schoolchildren hiding under their desks?

29 USA
ROCK & ROLL SINGER, 1935-1977
ELVIS

Why did WWII help create so many American suburbs?

WHY WAS ELVIS SUCH A SENSATION?

Before Elvis Presley arrived on the scene in 1955, adults and teenagers generally listened to the same music. Presley's music included elements of music from black performers, helping to create a faster, louder sound that was new to white audiences. His good looks and hip-swiveling moves helped make him a mega-star with a huge teenage following.

Suburbs are communities that spring up within driving distance of cities or other urban centers. When WWII ended in 1945, the U.S. economy grew strong. Millions of returning soldiers looked for places for their young families to live. Many of these soldiers got financial help from the government to buy homes. To meet this demand, builders developed huge areas of land near cities. Using mass-production techniques honed during the war, new communities could be built quickly

Why did hippies join protest marches in the 1960s?

As the Vietnam War escalated in the 1960s, the antiwar movement grew as well. Many groups protested, but one notable group was the hippies, who represented much of the music, art, and style we identify with the '60s. This young, idealistic movement rejected war, aggression, and violence, promoting peace and love instead. Also, many young men were being drafted to fight and die in a war they did not believe in. They had every reason to protest.

WHY DID CHRISTIAN BARNAARD BECOME FAMOUS AS A SURGEON?

On December 3, 1967, Barnaard, a South African surgeon, performed the world's first successful heart transplant. He took the heart from a person who had died in an accident. The recipient, Louis Washansky, lived for 18 days with his new heart. Since that pioneering effort, more than 100,000 hearts have been transplanted, with the majority of patients living for more than five years.

Why is Thurgood Marshall a civil rights hero?

For many years, Thurgood Marshall worked as a lawyer representing African-Americans who faced discrimination. He argued dozens of civil rights cases before the U.S. Supreme Court, most notably Brown vs. Board of Education, in 1954. As a result of Marshall's win, racial segregation was outlawed in schools. In 1967, the civil rights icon was named the first African-American Supreme Court justice.

Why did ping-pong help relations with China?

When China's Communist party took power in 1949, the United States cut off official diplomatic relations. Few Americans were allowed to visit China and the governments rarely communicated. Then, in 1971, American ping-pong players were invited to play in China, where the game is very popular. The invitation suggested a change in the attitudes of Chinese leaders and therefore helped pave the way for a visit from President Nixon. Without ping-pong, it might have taken many more years to break the diplomatic ice.

Why were there long lines for gasoline in the early 1970s?

During the 1973 Arab-Israeli War, the U.S. stood by its ally, Israel. In retaliation, oil-rich Arab nations cut off the flow of oil and gas to the U.S. Gas shortages quickly paralyzed the nation. Gas prices went up, while gas stations had very long lines. By the end of that year, oil started flowing again, teaching important lessons on the strategic value of energy, and greater energy independence, for the U.S. economy.

PUMPS CLOSED

WHY DID ALAN SHEPARD BRING A GOLF CLUB TO THE MOON?

Astronaut Alan Shepard loved golf. When he was chosen to take part in a Moon landing during the Apollo XVI mission in 1972, he brought his hobby with him. Shepard attached a golf club head to a hand tool and tucked golf balls in his spacesuit. During one of his walks on the Moon, he got out his club and hit a few balls, which went a long, long way in the Moon's light gravity.

121

Why was astronaut Sally Ride an American pioneer?

On June 18, 1983, Ride flew into orbit on the space shuttle *Challenger*, becoming the first American woman in space. (The first woman in space, Valentina Tereshkova of the Soviet Union, had orbited earth 20 years and 2 days before.) Ride's ride became an inspiration to millions of American girls, encouraging them to pursue science careers and their dreams.

Why did President Reagan say, "Mr. Gorbachev, tear down that wall"?

By 1987, Germany had been split into East and West for 42 years, and the Berlin Wall had been dividing the capital city for 26 years. That year, U.S. president Ronald Reagan spoke in Berlin. He challenged Soviet leader Mikhail Gorbachev to allow the wall to be taken down. It was finally destroyed in 1989, and the two Germanys were reunited into a unified country.

WHY WAS OCTOBER 19, 1987, CALLED BLACK MONDAY?

On that day, the U.S. stock market fell 22.6%. It was—and still is—the biggest one-day drop in U.S. history. On that day, billions of dollars disappeared. Millions of people lost vast sums of money as the value of their stocks plummeted.

Why did the U.S. lead a war against Iraq in 1991?

On August 2, 1990, Iraq invaded Kuwait, its much smaller neighbor to the south. Iraq wanted to capture Kuwait's enormous oil fields. Kuwait was an ally of the United States and European countries. In response, a U.S.-led military force launched Operation Desert Storm in 1991. Allied forces quickly liberated Kuwait, and Iraq soon agreed to give up its weapons of mass destruction and allow U.N. inspections and meet other demands.

Why was Nelson Mandela's election significant for South Africa?

Since 1948, the official policy of the South African government had been to completely separate white people from other races. This policy was called *apartheid*. Naturally, many rebelled against this racism. One rebel, Nelson Mandela, was jailed for 27 years for speaking out against apartheid. Years of worldwide pressure finally changed the policies of the government. In 1988, Mandela was released from prison. In 1989, he helped officially end apartheid policies. And in 1994, under a new constitution, Mandela became the first black president of South Africa, serving until 1999.

Why did the Supreme Court decide a presidential election?

The 2000 U.S. presidential election pitted Republican George W. Bush against Democrat Al Gore. On election night, all eyes were on Florida, because the winner of that state's electoral votes determined who would be president. About 180,000 ballots did not show a clear vote, so they were recounted by hand, which went on for weeks. Finally, the U.S. Supreme Court was called on to end the confusion. On the day the recount was stopped, Bush was ahead by 537 votes out of more than 6 million. Nationally, Gore got at least 500,000 more votes, but Bush had more electoral votes, so he won the election.

Why was President Obama's 2008 election historic?

When Barack Obama was elected to become the 44th President of the United State, he became the first African American to win the nation's highest office. Just 44 years earlier, many African-Americans were still being denied the right to vote. The 2008 election attracted at least 5 million more voters than any previous Presidential contest, and Obama won more votes than any candidate in U.S. history,

WWW.BARACKOBAMA.COM

CHANGE
WE CAN BELIEVE IN

WHY WERE COMPUTER USERS AFRAID OF JANUARY 1, 2000?

In 1999, tech experts feared what might happen when every computer's vital calendar changed from 12-31-99 to 01-01-00. Would computers process the year "00" as 1900, not 2000, and somehow malfunction? Many thought that would cause computers to crash. This wordwide fear was labeled Y2K, short for Year 2000. As it turned out, there were only a few digital glitches. Y2K was A-O.K.

Why was Japan's 2011 earthquake so destructive?

On March 11, 2011, an earthquake struck off the coast of Japan. The energy from the quake created a massive tsunami, or tidal wave, that swept across large parts of the island nation. It happened very suddenly and the surge of water was enormous, with 100-foot (91.4 m) waves smashing onto land. Entire cities were swept away, and more than 25,000 people were killed that fateful day.

WHY WOULD A MAN FALL 24 MILES ON PURPOSE?

On October 14, 2012, Felix Baumgartner, a world-famous Austrian skydiver, became the first person to break the speed of sound (about 750 mph/1,207 kph) without an airplane. He leaped from a capsule 24 miles (38.6 km) high, plummeting faster than 830 mph (1,335 kph) before parachuting safely to the ground.

Why was the election of Pope Francis a first for the Catholic Church?

When Cardinal Jorge Bergoglio of Argentina was elected as the 266th pope of the worldwide Roman Catholic Church, he became the first man from South America—or anywhere outside of Europe—to become pope.

SCIENCE

Why do helium balloons float?

Page 135

Why are there holes in Swiss cheese?

Cheese is made by adding bacteria to milk. Bacteria are single-celled organisms that multiply very fast. In the case of Swiss cheese, three types of bacteria are added. As the bacteria eat the milk, two types of bacteria produce lactic acid. The third type of bacteria lives off that lactic acid. As they eat it, they give off bubbles of carbon dioxide that form the holes.

Swiss cheese is called Emmental cheese in Switzerland.

Why are some bacteria good for you?

It's true that some bacteria can make you sick. But other types help keep you alive. Some of those "good" bacteria work inside your body to help you digest food. Other types live on your skin and in your mouth to protect you against the bad bacteria that can make you sick. Your body is a bacteria battleground!

WHY DO SOME CHEESES TASTE BETTER OVER TIME?

Age doesn't make everything better, but it often improves the taste of cheese. In some cheeses, aging allows the enzymes and bacteria to change and improve the taste and texture of the cheese. Each type of cheese requires a different aging period.

Good bacteria are prime ingredients in making cheese.

Why does rotting food smell bad?

Food rots when bacteria starts to eat away at it. Yeasts and mold can also decompose food. As these organisms eat the food, they give off various gases, which sometimes smell bad.

WHY DOES BREAD GET STALE?

Starch is a key part of bread. As soon as bread is finished baking, the soft starch starts to change. It pulls water from nearby molecules and starts becoming harder. That makes the bread itself get drier and harder . . . you know, stale.

Why is composting so good for the planet?

Composting is the process of turning food and yard waste back into rich soil that can grow food, flowers, and other plants. By making and using compost, gardeners are not only recycling food waste, they are improving the quality of the soil by adding nutrients. To create compost, gardeners add the waste and water to a bin, where microbes and worms break it into a black substance called *humus*.

129

Why does laundry detergent work?

The most important ingredients in laundry detergent are chemicals called surfactants. One end of a surfactant molecule is attracted to water, and the other end is attracted to dirt and grease. When you put detergent into a washing machine with dirty clothes, the dirt-loving end binds to the dirt. As the water swirls, it pulls the dirt away from the fabric.

Why does dish soap clean greasy plates?

Like laundry detergent, one end of the dish soap surfactant attaches itself to the grease on the dinner plate. The other end is attracted to the water. The force of water on this chain carries the grease off when the soap is rinsed away.

Detergent contains dirt-loving molecules.

WHY DO PEOPLE PUT BAKING SODA IN A REFRIGERATOR?

Baking soda is a very useful chemical called sodium bicarbonate. It is able to chemically neutralize odors caused by acids and other results of spoiled food. Putting an open container of baking soda in a fridge makes it less stinky.

Why is water called H_2O?

Hydrogen
H

drogen
H

+

Oxygen
O

=

A chemical reaction occurs when two or more substances interact. Water forms when two hydrogen atoms (H_2) interact with one oxygen atom (O). When scientists write that combination, it's H_2O.

Water's official name is dihydrogen monoxide.

Water
H_2O

Why does mixing vinegar and baking soda cause an explosion?

When you mix vinegar and baking soda, a chemical reaction takes place. The acetic acid in vinegar—which gives vinegar its sour taste—reacts with the sodium bicarbonate. Now you've got carbonic acid, which breaks down into carbon dioxide and water. The escaping carbon dioxide gas creates the bubbles you see overflowing like a gushing volcano. Don't do this without asking an adult for permission—and help cleaning up the mess.

WHY ARE SOLIDS, LIQUIDS, AND GASES DIFFERENT?

All three are states of matter, and matter can change states under pressure and in different temperatures. For instance, ice, water, and steam may seem different, but they're all the same matter: H_2O. A solid ice cube has particles that are held tightly in place and don't move around much. Water is a liquid, with particles that move around, but still stick together. Steam is a gas. Its fast-moving particles don't stay together.

WHY DOES SALT MELT ICE?

Water freezes into ice when the temperature falls below 32°F (0°C). But salt water freezes at a slightly lower temperature (28.4°F/−2°C). That's why people add salt to icy sidewalks and roads. It will melt the ice, at least until the temperature falls lower than the freezing point of salt water.

WHY DOES GUNPOWDER EXPLODE?

It doesn't. The chemicals in gunpowder burn very, very quickly. They release hot gases as they burn. If the gunpowder is packed into a tight space, there's no room for those gases to expand. When the pressure from the gas gets too strong, the container will explode outward. If the gunpowder isn't packed into a container, it will just burn very quickly, and the gases will escape without the *BOOM!*

Why are fireworks colorful?

Fireworks are packed with different chemicals. Each of the chosen chemicals produces a particular color when it explodes. Sodium makes fireworks burn yellow or gold. Copper creates blue colors. Barium produces green. And aluminum delivers the ever-popular silver and white sparkles.

This is how hockey players stop on the ice.

Why is ice slippery?

Although the question seems simple enough, scientists are still searching for an answer. They used to believe that ice under a skate is slippery because the skate's blade creates pressure that lowers the melting temperature of the ice surface. As the ice melts, the blade glides across a thin layer of water, which refreezes once the blade passes. Many scientists now believe that water molecules on the surface of ice vibrate faster because nothing is holding them down.

WHY DO ICE SKATES SCRAPE WHEN YOU STOP?

When a skater puts pressure on the edge of his skates, the blade's edges dig into the ice, increasing friction. That increase in friction creates drag, which slows the movement of the skater. At the same time, the sharp edges of the skates churn up ice particles that go flying.

WHY DOES A LIGHT BULB LIGHT UP?

Every time you turn on an incandescent light bulb, electricity flows into the bulb, heating a thin coil of metal wire, called a filament, to an incredibly hot 4,500°F (2,482°C). Hot metal glows bright. Meanwhile, the glass bulb's job is to protect the filament and keep away oxygen, which would make the filament burn out too quickly inside the bulb.

Why are remote control **copters** so easy to fly?

A quadcopter uses four propellers, each connected to its own motor. The remote controls let you change the speed of each motor. So, if you want the copter to roll to the right, your remote would speed up the left-side motors and slow down the right-side motors. Because quadcopters have electronic stabilization systems, they stay balanced.

WHY DO YOU NEED SO MANY PEOPLE TO HOLD A PARADE BALLOON?

Some special character balloons can be more than six stories tall, floating above huge crowds. A strong wind can blow against the balloons and set them free—it has happened before! It often requires crews of up to 90 people to make sure these balloons stay down to earth.

Why do helium balloons float?

Helium is a gas that is lighter than air. A balloon rises because the helium displaces, or pushes away, the heavier air around the balloon. This is known as buoyancy. Once a helium balloon rises into the thin, cold upper atmosphere, the pressure causes it to pop and fall to earth.
It's dangerous for sea creatures, birds, and other animals to eat a deflated balloon, so don't let yours float away.

The helium in balloons is lighter than air.

WHY IS AN ARROW AERODYNAMIC?

An arrow is an ancient creation. The head is a weighted, pointed triangle that cuts through the air's resistance. It's strong enough to pierce a target. The feathers, or fletching, help the arrow stay stable and remain on course. In between is the long shaft of the arrow. If the shaft is not stiff enough, or is too stiff, it will affect your accuracy. Bullseye!

Why do bees make honey?

Honey is food for bees. To make the sticky stuff, honeybees gather nectar, a sweet liquid produced by flowers. A single bee might visit 50 or 100 flowers each time it looks for food. Many honeybees gather nectar together, while other bees transform it to honey in the hive. They store the tasty food for the months when flowers are not blooming.

Why do bees dance?

Bees dance as a way to communicate with each other. Scout bees, for example, look for flower beds bursting with nectar and pollen. If they find one, they fly to the hive and do a dance that tells the other bees what they found. Some bees also dance a "round dance" to announce that food is near the hive.

As many as 70,000 bees can live in one hive.

Bees help create new plants.

WHY ARE BEES GOOD FOR FLOWERS?

Bees fly from flower to flower to collect nectar for their honey. Along their journey, they end up carrying pollen from the male part of some flowers (the stamen) to the female part of other flowers (the pistil). These little matchmakers are vital in creating new plants. The process is called pollination. After the bee leaves pollen on a flower, the flower creates a seed. From that seed a new plant can grow.

Why can **some animals see in the dark?**

All animals see by receiving light into their eyes. Some animals have evolved eyes that receive light even in very low levels. These animals can move through the dark when other animals might have trouble seeing. They have a special layer in their eyes that reflects light called the *tapetum lucidum*. It is responsible for the eerie shining eyes you may have seen in nighttime photos of dogs, cats, and other animals.

WHY CAN MANY ANIMALS HEAR SOUNDS THAT WE CAN'T?

Sound travels in waves through the air. Because many animals have ears that are larger or more flexible than ours, their ears receive more sound waves than human ears. Also, the inner ear parts of many animals are able to hear high-pitched, higher frequency sound waves that humans can't.

Why are **certain small animals deadly?**

Some animals, including several snakes, spiders, frogs, and lizards, produce poisons or venoms that can kill. Poisons are often deadly when touched or swallowed. Venoms can kill when injected into you, which a rattlesnake's fangs will do. Most often, venoms are used to kill prey for the animal to eat. Other times, poison or venom is used in defense. It's a jungle out there . . . watch where you walk!

How do clouds form?

As warm air rises, it becomes colder. Gradually, the water vapor in the air turns into very small drops of water. The molecules in the water grab hold of tiny bits of dust, pollen, and other types of pollution. The water molecules condense onto these particles and collect together. All those molecules together make a cloud. When clouds become heavy, they release water back to the earth as rain, sleet, snow, or hail.

Why does snow fall?

Snow begins its life as an ice crystal. Ice crystals form when a cloud's temperature is below freezing (32°F/0°C). If the air temperature below the cloud is also below freezing, the crystals cling together and fall to the ground as snowflakes, thanks to gravity.

WHY ARE SOME SNOWFLAKES SO BIG?

The average snowflake is made of crystals that total about half an inch (1.3 cm) across. Sometimes many separate ice crystals stick together, creating a snowflake that can measure more than 4 inches (10 cm) across.

4" (10 cm)

Why is the **Equator** hotter than the North and South Poles?

The same amount of sunlight hits the Earth all over. However, the sun's rays fall more directly on the equator—the bulging center of the Earth's sphere—than at its poles. As a result, equatorial Africa and South America are much warmer than the Arctic or Antarctica.

Equator

WHY DO WE USE A BAROMETER?

Just as a thermometer measures temperature, a barometer measures air pressure. When the barometer shows high pressure, that means the weather is generally clear. When the barometer goes down, the chances for a storm go up!

This lion lives in Kenya, a very hot African nation on the Equator.

WHY IS IT COLDER AT THE TOP OF A MOUNTAIN?

Hiking up a mountain is cool, and as you climb, it gets even cooler! The temperature of air is determined in part by the pressure it is under. As you rise up further from sea level, the air pressure gets lower and lower . . . and so does the air temperature.

Lower air pressure causes lower temperatures.

139

Why do leaves change color?

Trees make their own food through a process called photosynthesis. During photosynthesis, trees use the sun's light to turn water and carbon dioxide into oxygen and a kind of sugar called glucose. Trees use glucose as food for energy. During the winter, there is not enough sunlight for the trees to make chlorophyll, the substance that's needed for photosynthesis. Without chlorophyll, the leaves' green color fades. Depending on the type of tree, the leaves then become orange, red, yellow, or brown.

When trees stop making food, leaves fall.

Why do leaves fall?

As sunlight decreases in the autumn, the hollow tubes that carry fluids into and out of a leaf begin to close. As that happens, a layer of cells forms at the base of the leaf stem, separating the stem from the tree. When a breeze comes along, the leaf falls.

WHY IS GRASS GREEN?

Like almost all green plants, grass is green because it is filled with chlorophyll. Chlorophyll is the green pigment that absorbs sunlight during photosynthesis.

Why do **some** plants eat bugs?

In some environments, plants do not have all the nutrients in the soil they need to live. Some plants adapted and developed a solution. Along with food from the soil, these plants evolved to eat bugs. By trapping and consuming bugs, the plants are able to get enough nutrients in places where most other plants can not survive.

WHY DO SOME BUSHES HAVE FUZZY LEAVES?

The fuzz may be pretty, but it also has a purpose. The tiny bristles keep moisture trapped on the leaves, which is helpful in sunny and dry places. Lighter colored bristles also reflect sunlight, which helps the plants keep cool in a bright environment.

Why can **some plants** grow without soil?

Plants called *Tillandsia*, or air plants, evolved to survive without roots that need to be in soil. They can get all their nutrients through their leaves. They do need a little water, which they get from mist in the air. Other plants, which float in water, can also live and grow without ever requiring soil.

Why does a pencil write?

The material inside a pencil is a soft mineral called graphite. As the pencil moves across the paper, tiny bits of graphite rub off, leaving a trail wherever the pencil has gone. Since the 1500s, people have used graphite to make marks on paper. Though the first pencils were called lead pencils, relatively few actually contained lead.

WHY DOES AN ERASER ERASE?

When the question is "What is 2+2?" and you have left tiny graphite particles in the shape of a 5, what do you need? A math lesson and a rubber eraser. The friction of rubbing the eraser on the paper makes the particles in the rubber stickier than the paper. The pencil's particles will leave the paper and stick to the eraser instead. (P.S. The correct answer is 4.)

Rubber has been used as material for erasers since 1770.

What makes **crayons different colors?**

Crayons are made of paraffin wax. The wax is basically clear, which allows crayon manufacturers to add powders called pigments. Each pigment changes the wax to a different color.

Crayons are colored wax.

WHY DO BALLPOINT PENS KEEP INK FROM BEING MESSY?

At the end of a ballpoint pen is a tiny rolling ball. It acts as a kind of cork, keeping the ink in the tube above. When you press down on the pen, the ball moves, releasing ink that flows around the ball and onto the paper as you write or draw. When you ease the pressure and stop writing, the "cork" plugs up the tube to keep ink from leaking out.

Why are some markers washable?

In 1953, an inventor put a felt wick on top of a glass bottle of ink and the Magic Marker was born. So were inky messes, which is why washable markers were developed using a solvent that can be cleaned with soap and water. Permanent markers, which write on many different surfaces, like glass, plastic, wood, and metal, use a solvent that water won't clean up.

Why is **glue sticky?**

The chemicals in glue do two things at the same time. *Adhesion* lets the glue hold objects together. *Cohesion* lets the glue hold on to itself. First, the glue's adhesive properties stick to surfaces by seeping into the cracks and holes of an object. Next, the cohesive properties harden and lock onto that surface.

WHY IS DUCT TAPE STRONGER THAN CLEAR TAPE?

Clear tape is a thin layer of plastic with sticky adhesive glue on one side. Duct tape is much thicker. It has several layers of material, including a waterproof coating of polyethylene, a strong, cotton mesh middle layer, and a third layer that is sticky on one side. When it comes to making tape stronger, three layers are better than one.

Glue has two properties that make it sticky.

WHY ARE RUBBER BANDS SO FLEXIBLE?

Rubber bands stretch because their molecules bond together into long, twisty chains called polymers. Pulling a rubber band causes the polymers to untwist and straighten. But release the rubber band, and the polymers will return to their original form. Unless you pulled too hard, then . . . snap!

Why can you **erase** a whiteboard?

Whiteboards will wipe clean if you use special dry erase markers. These markers are made with particular chemicals and dyes that won't stick to the board's surface. The board itself is specially treated so that it will not absorb anything.

Why did **sticky notes** take a long time to invent?

In 1968, a chemist tried to create a super-strong adhesive. However, the formula he made was only a little bit sticky. Years later, another chemist used that same formula to make a bulletin board. It worked, except no one wanted a sticky bulletin board. Finally, other workers came up with the idea of putting the not-very-sticky stuff on the paper we call sticky notes, which first appeared in 1977. That's the power of teamwork.

TECHNOLOGY

Why does an airplane fly?

Page 155

Why does binary computer code use ones and zeroes?

The circuits that run computers include many millions of tiny switches called transistors. They can be turned on or off by an electric pulse. The programs that run computers instantly read those pulses as code. The 1s in computer code turn a transistor on, the 0s turn it off. By combining a long string of 1s and 0s, the program creates words, numbers, commands, and instructions that perform the operations we expect from a computer.

Why do most web pages begin with HTTP?

The Internet connects billions of computers to one another. How do you find the one you're looking for? Your computer's browser is a program that will do the hunting . . . if you give it the right address. Web addresses are standardized so that all computers can read them. That standard is called Hypertext Transfer Protocol (HTTP). Those letters tell the browser that what follows will be an address on the World Wide Web.

Why do we type on a QWERTY keyboard?

The typewriter was invented nearly 150 years ago. Through years of trial and error, including suggestions from Morse Code operators, the QWERTY layout was patented in 1878. It is not the most efficient layout, but it is now so common and familiar, no one has successfully replaced it.

WHY DOES E-MAIL USE THE @ KEY?

A computer scientist named Ray Tomlinson developed the first working e-mail system in 1971. He needed a symbol to separate a name from an address. He looked at his keyboard and found the answer: @ means "at." It's been @ the center of e-mail addresses ever since.

Why were old computer monitors so fat?

Older monitors didn't use tiny LCDs or LEDs to make an image. They used old-fashioned, glass picture tubes, causing a foot-high (0.3 m) monitor to need to be as much as two feet deep. Monitors also got hotter than today's machines and needed larger fans and more ventilation inside to stay cool.

WHY ARE PEOPLE SOMETIMES ASKED TO TURN OFF CELL PHONES ON A PLANE?

For many years, people could not use portable devices at all during flights. There was concern about phone signals interfering with airplane equipment. Also, people were ignoring the safety messages. But times and tech changed, now more airlines allow it once a plane reaches 10,000 feet.

WHY ARE TWEETS ONLY 140 CHARACTERS?

When someone sends a tweet on Twitter, it's short. Blame the original, not-smart phone screens that could only display 160 characters at a time. Twitter, which arrived during this time, chose 140 characters to make sure an entire message could be seen on any single small screen.

Why are cell phone networks called 4G and 3G?

The 3G label is short for third generation network, while 4G means . . . take one good guess. Each generation of networks improves on the previous one. 3G networks are more advanced than the previous network. For example, you can send large amounts of data on either network, but 4G networks are faster than 3G. Next up: 5G, and it might be coming soon.

Why do **viruses** harm computers?

A computer virus is a nasty computer code that can disrupt or destroy computers and networks. Don't click on links or attachments you don't already trust. A virus can enter your computer that way, crashing programs, freezing hard drives, and worst of all, surrendering vital private data to cybercriminals. Anti-virus programs can help, but it's important to be very careful.

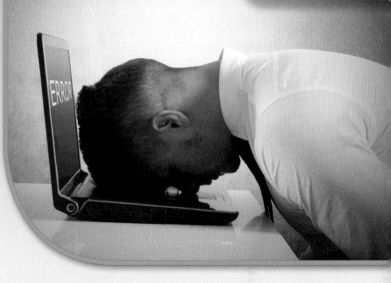

Why can't **iPhones** and **Android phones** use the same apps?

Android phones and iPhones have been developed differently, with separate operating systems that each speak a different computer language. The apps you run on different phones may look alike, but their programming can be quite different.

Why are **some places** "out of range" for cell phones?

Cell phone signals depend on large cell towers that pass along their signal from place to place. In some places, the towers are too far apart to let signals connect. In remote areas, there might be no towers at all. Dead zone, dead phone.

When the radio was first invented, it was used more like a telephone. Radio operators chose names, numbers, or words to identify themselves. As the number of radio operators increased, so did confusion and conflict. That's when government officials ruled that each operator—and soon, each radio and TV station—had to have its own call letters.

There are about 44,000 radio stations in the world.

Why do U.S. TV and radio station names start with W or K?

You can find WABC in New York, and KABC in Los Angeles. These call letters are a station's official name. By the 1920s, stations had grown in such great numbers that a system was needed to know who was broadcasting from where. In 1928, the Mississippi River became the dividing line for U.S. stations, with eastern stations beginning with W, and western stations starting with K. Canadian stations start with C, and Mexican stations begin with X.

WHY CAN SATELLITE RADIO STATIONS REACH SO MANY PEOPLE?

The most common radio signals are sent from towers. The power of those signals fades with distance from the tower, and the signals can be blocked by hills or mountains. On the other hand, signals sent from satellites in space can reach huge areas. Almost nothing can block the signal from reaching your radio except, of course, flying saucers.

Why are some TVs LED and others are LCD?

TVs that are LCD (*liquid crystal display*) use small fluorescent lamps to light up liquid crystals behind the screen. LED stands for *light emitting diodes*—those are the little bright lights found everywhere, from car tail lights to the "on" light on your electronic devices. In an LED TV, individual LEDs light the crystals behind the glass. The benefits of LED technology include a better picture, thinner TVs, and less overall energy used.

WHY CAN'T BLU-RAY DISCS PLAY IN A REGULAR DVD PLAYER?

Blu-ray discs aren't compatible with DVD players because their technology is different. On DVDs, a red laser reads the disc. Blu-ray is named for its blue LED light, which reads the disc's much larger, higher-quality audio and video files. Fortunately, a Blu-ray player can play older DVDs.

HDTVs are quickly replacing standard TVs.

Why does HDTV look more realistic than standard TV?

Each TV picture is made up of millions of dots, called pixels (short for picture elements). A standard TV image has 480 lines of pixels from top to bottom. That looked fine until high definition (HD) screens came along, displaying 720 lines, or 1,080 lines, and now, with 4K technology, 2,160 lines per screen. So many more pixels bring a much clearer, sharper picture.

Why do cars and trucks need gasoline?

Gasoline creates power because it is explosive. Inside the engine, the gas is sparked, causing hundreds of small explosions every minute. Each tiny blast moves one of the engine's pistons up and down, creating a lot of power. The pistons turn a crankshaft that moves the vehicle's wheels. Now you're moving, and it all started with a little bit of gas!

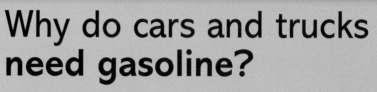

Why do some cars get better gas mileage than others?

Lighter cars and smaller cars need less energy to operate. Also, better engines are now being built to burn less gasoline than older cars. Some cars are hybrids, meaning they use electricity as well as gasoline. Fully electric cars don't use any gas at all. In the U.S., cars are supposed to be designed to average 54 miles (87 km) per gallon by 2025.

Why are there different kinds of tires?

There are different tires for different jobs. Standard car tires are used for streets and highways. Snow tires have wider, deeper treads to grip snowy, icy roads. Tires for trucks that haul through dirt, mud, and rocks need to be very tough in tough conditions. Some Formula 1 race car tires have almost no tread to increase grip. And tires on trucks that build roads can measure more than 13 feet (4 m) tall!

Why does an airplane fly?

When a propeller pulls a plane forward, air moves across the top of the wing faster than it moves below the wing. That causes less air pressure on top of the wing than below. This creates lift, which causes the plane to take off. Once the plane has taken off, lift allows it to ride along the air much like a surfer rides on waves. The Wright Brothers put these facts to work when their heavier-than-air machine first flew for 12 seconds on December 17, 1903.

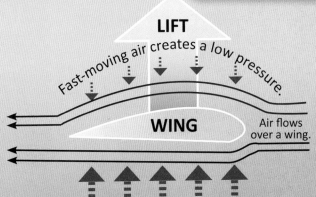

LIFT

Fast-moving air creates a low pressure.

WING

Air flows over a wing.

Slower-moving air creates high pressure that pushes upward, causing the lift necessary for flight.

Orville Wright was the first person to successfully fly an engine-powered airplane.

Why do **rotors** make a helicopter fly?

On a helicopter, the lift is produced by the blades, also called rotors. Air rushes over the top rotors just as it does over an airplane's wings. The spinning rotors let the vehicle move straight up and down, and even hover in mid-air. Though helicopters are connected to giant spinning blades, they don't spin in circles, thanks to the stabilizing effect of the small vertical rotor near the tail. That gives the pilot control of the craft.

WHY ARE JETS SO FAST?

You know how a balloon flies around a room when you untie the knot, forcing out air? Jets work on a similar principle, except they never run out of air. Rotating blades suck air into the powerful jet engine up front. The air is mixed with fuel, ignited, and ejected from the back with tremendous force.

155

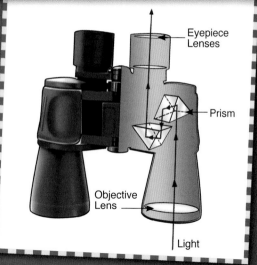

Eyepiece Lenses

Prism

Objective Lens

Light

Why can I see faraway objects with binoculars?

When optical lenses are curved (like in a magnifying glass), the objects you see through them can appear closer than they actually are. When you look through two lenses in a row, the effect makes objects seem *much* closer. Prisms between the lenses make sure the image is not flipped. And unlike with a telescope, you can use both eyes.

WHY DO I SEE MY REFLECTION IN A MIRROR?

You see your reflection because light bounces off the polished surface of a mirror and reflects back to you. If the mirror is not smooth, or flat, light will not bounce evenly, and your reflection will be distorted. Most mirrors are made from thin layers of reflective aluminum or silver covered in glass.

The first microscope was built around 1590 by Hans and Zacharias Jansen.

WHY DO MICROSCOPES LET ME SEE EXTREMELY SMALL OBJECTS?

In an optical microscope, a light shines upward through a series of small lenses. The light that passes through each lens magnifies, or increases, the image created by the light. The image is then further magnified by a second lens in the eyepiece. The user can adjust the focus or the magnification by using different lenses.

Why are optical and digital camera zooms different?

A zoom lens makes faraway objects appear closer to the camera, much like looking through a telescope. Optical zooms stick out of the camera. When they zoom in or out, they rearrange the position of multiple lenses, changing the distance between them. A digital zoom is a lower quality trick of a camera's software. The object you see may look larger, but the camera is just cropping and expanding the image. It would be far better to take your camera's best possible photo and adjust it later, using your computer.

WHY DO CAMERAS NEED A FLASH WHEN TAKING PICTURES IN THE DARK?

A camera captures light as it bounces off of objects. When it's dim or dark, the flashing light throws extra light over the area so the camera can record the photo. Watch out for red eyes!

Why do selfies make my arms look big?

Even though your selfies make you look like one of the Fantastic Four, it's not your camera's fault. The lens on your phone takes a picture of everything it sees. Since your arms are quite a lot closer to the camera lens than the rest of you, they look bigger and wider to the camera. People use selfie sticks to avoid this trick of perspective.

157

Why did riverboats have paddle wheels?

Paddle wheels are like swim fins for a boat. These 19th century inventions powered the first watercraft that had engines. Steam engines turn the circular paddles to move the ships through the water. They became outdated when underwater propellers proved more efficient. They're used mainly for the flat, still water of lakes, ponds, and rivers. They are still popular with tourists.

Why did the first cars look like horse carriages?

When early automakers needed something to put their engines in, they naturally chose the vehicles they were already driving. A nickname for early cars was "horseless carriages." Car engine strength is still measured in horsepower.

Why do old trains make so much steam?

Steam locomotives chugged across America for more than a century. To run the engine, coal was burned to heat water in a boiler. The steam then moved the pistons up and down and up again. Boiling water isn't an exact science, and too much steam could be created. Any extra steam got pushed out with a *whoosh* to avoid an explosion.

Why did Alexander Graham Bell invent the telephone?

The Scottish-born inventor actually created the telephone accidentally. He was looking for a way to invent a better telegraph machine that used sound instead of the dots and dashes of Morse Code. On March 10, 1876, Bell and his assistant, Thomas A. Watson, were working in separate rooms. Bell shouted into a prototype, "Mr. Watson—come here—I want to see you." And it worked. As a comedian once said, it's a good thing the man's name wasn't Alexander Graham Siren, or it would be very loud when you got a phone call!

WHY DID OLD TELEPHONES COME IN TWO PARTS?

Known as the candlestick phone, this style, designed by Bell in 1892, stayed popular until the 1930s. Because the earpiece and mouthpiece were still new technology, they were separated. Users spoke into the microphone on the upright part while holding the corded speaker to their ear.

Why did the telegraph change the world?

Up through the early 1830s, writing was one of the only ways to communicate with distant people. Sending a letter could take weeks or months. Then, in the mid-1830s, Samuel Morse invented a system that sent electric signals along long wires. Using an alphabet made up of dashes and dots—Morse Code—those signals could be translated into words. Soon, people could communicate across town, across the country, and across oceans.

159

WHY DO DOCTORS USE X-RAYS?

Viewing an X-ray photo lets doctors diagnose and treat injuries and illnesses. X-rays are a kind of radiation that can go through clothing and skin, but not bones. The rays are used to create an image of bones and other body parts that can be captured on film.

Some technicians take dozens of X-rays a day!

WHY DO HEALTH WORKERS LEAVE THE ROOM DURING AN X-RAY?

X-rays are electromagnetic radiation. A few X-rays in a lifetime are not harmful, so patients simply wear a lead protector. X-ray technicians, however, take many X-rays a day. To avoid so much radioactive exposure, they step into a shielded room to take the X-ray. It's for their own safety!

Why is an MRI different from an X-ray?

A magnetic resonance imaging (MRI) machine uses magnetic fields and radio waves instead of X-rays to make images of a body's inner workings. Powerful magnets in the machine send out waves that pass through the body and provide a helpful picture. MRIs are used to find medical conditions that X-rays just can't see.

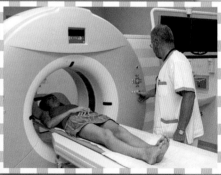

Why can robots improve people's lives?

People who lose limbs can now be helped by robotic prosthetics that connect to their nervous systems. As technology improves, increasingly subtle electric impulses from a person's body will be able to be received, and understood, by these sophisticated limbs.

Why can a doctor diagnose you from far away?

Thanks to live video streaming, many patients consult with their doctors using their laptops or tablets. Doctors can see test results, talk about the symptoms, and even perform simple visual examinations. But they still can't give you a shot through your iPad . . . yet.

Why can 3-D printing save lives?

Scientists are working on creating body parts using custom 3-D printing. The goal is to soon be able to easily print bones, tracheas, ear parts, or other solid human parts that can be custom made especially for each patient. Next time someone asks you to lend an ear, tell them to print their own.

161

SPORTS

Why do soccer players "bend" the ball?

Page 178

Why are baseball fields different sizes?

While the rules of Major League Baseball spell out the exact size of the infield, the outfield is a different story. Each ballpark has different outfield dimensions. Often the park was designed to fit in crowded urban places. According to the rules, the distance from home plate to the nearest fence in fair territory must be at least 250 feet (76.2 m). Some teams use their field's measurements to their advantage. Because Yankee Stadium's right-field fence is only 314 feet (95.7 m) from home plate, the New York Yankees often put strong left-handed batters in their lineup. The left-field fence at Boston's Fenway Park is only 310 feet (94.5 m) from the batter, which is great news for right-handed sluggers. Meanwhile, Houston's Minute Maid Park has a centerfield that is baseball's longest, measuring 430 feet (131 m) from home plate.

Outfields vary, but baseball infields are all the same size.

WHY ARE SOME TENNIS COURTS RED?

Tennis is played on several different surfaces. The most popular is called hardcourt, a form of cement. These are often painted green or blue, with white lines. Grass is sometimes used as well, most famously at Wimbledon in England. But at the site of the famous French Open (and other places), the court is made of hard-packed limestone covered with a thin layer of red brick dust. These are called "clay courts," even though they aren't made out of clay.

WHY WAS THE ZAMBONI MACHINE INVENTED?

After 20 minutes of hockey action (the length of a period in a game), the rink's ice surface is a mess. The players' skates have cut grooves in the ice and turned it into a rough, uneven surface. Smoothing it out used to take a long time. In the early 1940s, inventor Frank Zamboni created a machine that smoothes the ice in minutes! First, a thin blade in the machine shaves off the top layer of ice. Water squirts down to clean the ice. A vacuum sucks up the debris. The final step is to lay down a clean film of water that forms smooth ice . . . until the next face-off!

Why is **basketball** played on wooden courts?

For the truest bounce, the nicest spring, and the longest wear, wood is the best surface for basketball courts. The game was played on a wood floor, after all, back in 1891 when it was invented at a Massachusetts YMCA by Dr. James Naismith. You can play outdoors on rough and uneven asphalt or dirt, but players playing indoors on a wood floor know just where the ball will bounce.

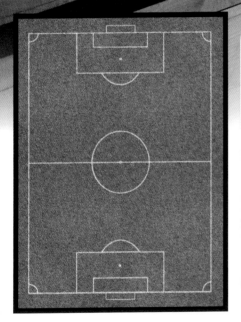

WHY IS A SOCCER FIELD CALLED A PITCH?

This term is most common in Great Britain, but more and more Americans are picking it up. The word *pitch* is also used for cricket fields, and that's where it comes from. When soccer started in the 1860s, people often played on cricket pitches, which became soccer pitches. Pounding the cricket wickets into the ground was called "pitching the stumps," similar to pitching a camping tent. Over time, the word has come to be used for the whole field.

Why are **some golf** courses called links?

Golf was first played in the 1600s on rough, rolling sheep meadows along the coast of Scotland. Those areas of land were called, in the Scots language, *hlincs*. Today, only courses that are created on similar stretches of land can properly be called links courses, but many golfers casually use the term to refer to any place they play!

WHY DOES A BASKETBALL RIM HAVE A NET?

What would happen if they didn't? If a shot sailed cleanly through the metal rim officials, players, and fans might not always be able to see whether a shot went in. The net is designed to slow down the ball to help make sure that all the points count!

Why is a basketball orange?

Until the late 1950s, basketballs were dark brown. College coach Paul "Tony" Hinkle thought that fans and players had a hard time seeing the ball against wooden floors. Working with Spalding, a company that made basketballs, Hinkle tried out a brighter color, and just about everyone was seeing orange by 1958.

Why do basketball players dribble?

Bouncing the ball is called dribbling, which was not always a part of basketball. In the late 1800s, players only ran with the ball. That led to rough play, so the rules were changed and players could only pass the ball but not run with it. That got too boring. In 1901, the rules changed again to allow a single bounce, but that didn't speed things up. By 1909, players could dribble the ball as much as they wanted, but they couldn't stop and then start again . . . that's called double dribbling. Dribbling is now a key part of the game, giving a player a way to move around the court with the ball while keeping it away from defenders.

Why is a basketball hoop 10 feet off the ground?

That height—10 feet (3.1 m)—is where James Naismith put the hoops when he invented basketball in 1891. Naismith created the sport by attaching peach baskets to a low balcony above the gym floor at the YMCA in Springfield, Massachusetts. The sport has honored the same regulation basket height ever since.

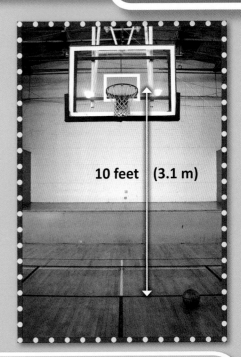

10 feet (3.1 m)

WHY WERE BASKETBALL PLAYERS SOMETIMES CALLED CAGERS?

In the early days of basketball, the first team to put their hands on the ball when it flew out of bounds and into the stands was given possession of the ball. So when the ball went off the court, the players rushed for it. In the scramble, fans often got hurt. To keep the ball in play at all times and prevent accidents, many arenas put a chicken-wire cage around the court. The cages were removed in the 1920s when the out-of-bounds rule was changed. Now if the ball goes out, play stops and the team that touched the ball last loses possession.

Players use jump shots to score more points in basketball.

WHY IS THE JUMP SHOT SO EFFECTIVE?

Before there was a jump shot, there was the set shot, where players plant their feet on the court and shoot the ball with one or both hands. Eventually, players developed the jump shot, which is made by releasing the ball from above the head while jumping. It proved to be more accurate from long range, in part because a jump shot puts a backspin on the ball. This helps direct the ball into the basket when it hits the backboard. Fans think it's more fun to watch, too!

167

Why do football players put **black grease under their eyes?**

Sunlight bouncing off players' cheekbones can sometimes create glare. To fight that, players first smeared burnt cork and, later, black grease beneath their eyes. Today, most players stick on strips of black adhesive tape for the same purpose. Many players wear the tape during night games because they like how ferocious they look!

WHY ARE HELMETS INFLATED WITH AIR?

The best way to protect a football player's head is with a properly fitting helmet. To make sure that each helmet fits a particular head, most styles have an air valve on the outside. After the player puts his or her helmet on, air is pumped in to pads lining the inside of the shell. The pads inflate to form-fit to the player's head, making the helmet as safe and effective as possible.

Why do **football coaches cover their mouths during games?**

They don't want their opponents to spy on them! Football coaches wear headsets to communicate with assistant coaches who sit high above the field. The coaches up above pass information to the coach on the field, who then makes the final decisions for the team. While the coach on the field is talking, he covers his or her mouth to make sure no lip-readers can intercept and pass secrets to the other team!

Why did the forward pass change the game of football?

In the early years of football passing the ball was against the rules. Instead, like rugby, its cousin, football was all about brutal packs of players running with the ball. Many injuries and even deaths occurred. In 1905, President Theodore Roosevelt met with college officials and said they had to change the game or he'd ban it. The rules were changed to allow players to pass the ball from behind the line of scrimmage. As teams spread across the field by using passes, there were fewer huge and dangerous pileups.

WHY DO HOLDERS SPIN THE LACES FORWARD?

A leather football has a row of laces to seal its rubber insides and provide a grip for passers. But laces pose a problem for kickers, who claim that if they boot the laces, their kicks won't go straight. That's why the holder who catches the snap always tries to spin the ball so that the laces are aimed at the target: the goalposts.

Why is the Green Bay NFL team called the Packers?

The Green Bay Packers were first owned by two different meat packing companies. As owners of the team, they got to pick the name, so they chose Packers. Although both companies

Why is a **touchdown** worth six points?

American football evolved from rugby football, a game that uses much more kicking. So when American football began in the late 1800s, kicked goals were more important than touchdowns. As American football players began doing more running and less kicking, scoring touchdowns became harder, so their value was increased in 1912, from 5 points to 6, to create higher scores.

Why do **Canadian** football teams play on a larger field?

Blame rugby again! The Canadian Football League plays a game very similar to the American version, but on a field that is larger. Both games evolved from English rugby, but the Canadian version kept more rugby-like rules about kicking and scoring. And while the American field shrank to 100 yards (91.4 m) long, the Canadian version remains about the same size as the larger rugby field, 110 yards (101 m).

WHY DID TWO WOMEN MAKE FOOTBALL HISTORY?

In 2015, Sarah Thomas became the first woman to work full time as an NFL official, working during games as a line judge. In early 2016, Kathryn Smith was named the special teams quality control coach for the Buffalo Bills, the first full-time female coach in league history.

WHY IS THE SUPER BOWL MVP TROPHY NAMED FOR PETE ROZELLE?

Pete Rozelle was the NFL Commissioner from 1960 to 1989. He played a huge part in making the league and the Super Bowl into the huge successes they are today. He was the first to get the league national TV contracts, and he helped create the Super Bowl in 1967. After his death, the league named the Most Valuable Player trophy after Rozelle.

SWELL
FOOTBALL GREATS
Pete Rozelle
COMMISSIONER

SUPER BOWL 50
#SB50   FEBRUARY 7, 2016

Why is the NFL championship game called the Super Bowl?

The first two championship games between the original AFL and NFL were not called the Super Bowl, but had another, longer, more boring name (see left). Lamar Hunt, the one-time owner of the Kansas City Chiefs, saw his daughter playing with a toy superball. Many college teams played in "bowl" games after their seasons, so Hunt combined the two ideas into "Super Bowl." Clearly, the name stuck.

Why was the first Super Bowl played?

In 1966, the American Football League merged with the National Football League. To determine the overall champion of this new union, the first AFL-NFL Championship Game was held on January 15, 1967, in Los Angeles, California. The Green Bay Packers of the NFL (now the NFC) beat the Kansas City Chiefs of the AFL (now the AFC), 35-10. The game was later renamed the Super Bowl and remains pro football's championship contest.

Why is an **American championship** called the **World Series?**

When two top baseball teams played for a national championship in 1884, a newspaper trying to make that series seem even more impressive named it the World's Championship—even though no other countries were taking part. In 1903, when Major League Baseball started its official championship, it called the event the World Series, too, even though both teams were American. Today, Major League Baseball's "world" includes Canada, but no other nations. It's worth noting that since 2006, three truly international baseball series have been held, using the more accurate name of World Baseball Classic.

Why do **baseballs have stitches?**

Waxed cotton stitches hold together the two figure-eight-shaped pieces of leather that form the outside of a baseball. That outside holds together a very stuffed interior! Hundreds of yards of wool and cotton thread are wound in a tight sphere around the center core of rubber and cork. All that soft stuff turns into a hard ball!

Why does a curveball curve?

High pressure

Path of ball

Direction of spin

Low pressure

Direction of airflow over ball

A talented baseball pitcher can make a baseball change direction in mid-air, thanks to skill—and physics. To curve the ball, the pitcher twists his wrist as he releases it, creating spin—as much as 30 times a second. As the spinning ball travels through the air, the spin creates low air pressure beneath the ball and high pressure above it. The ball moves down toward the lower pressure. But here's the key: air moving over the ball's raised stitching directs that movement of the ball even more sharply in the direction of the spin. This causes the ball to curve toward one side, giving the batter an unwelcome surprise!

WHY ARE ALUMINUM BATS MORE DANGEROUS THAN WOOD BATS?

Metal baseball bats can be dangerous, because baseballs fly off a metal bat faster than off a wood bat. The aluminum bat's shell actually narrows as it contacts the ball. As it springs back into shape, it adds more force to the motion of the ball than a wood bat. That faster-moving ball can be hard to avoid.

Why is the Baseball Hall of Fame in Cooperstown, New York?

In 1903, a special committee declared that baseball had been invented in 1839 by Abner Doubleday, who later became a Union Army general. The story was that the general drew up the rules on a field in Cooperstown, New York. The catch? The story wasn't true, misleading people for decades. In 1936, when plans were made for a new Baseball Hall of Fame, the natural choice was the fictional home of the game . . . which you can still visit today.

173

Why was 1973 a big year for Little League?

Until 1973, girls were not allowed to play Little League Baseball. That year, thanks to some critical court rulings, Little League changed its policy and let girls join teams. The following year, it also created Little League Softball to help more girls learn a sport they could continue in high school and beyond.

WHY WAS SOFTBALL INVENTED?

Softball was invented by mistake! In 1887, a bunch of men were horsing around at a club after attending a football game. One of them tossed a boxing glove at another fan, who whacked it with a stick. The glove went flying! Watching this, sportswriter John Hancock grabbed the glove and wrapped it tight with string. Moments later, the first softball game was underway. Hancock later created more rules for the game, and soon clubs were playing the game indoors and out. The game was known by various names, including mushball, until it was first called softball by a YMCA group in 1926.

Why are **advanced baseball stats called Sabermetrics?**

Baseball fans love numbers, and baseball has statistics for just about everything. In 1971, a group of baseball history fans formed the Society for American Baseball Research. In recent years, more of the group's members have focused on using computers and advanced math to create new and more complicated baseball stats. Those new stats, which have greatly changed how fans and experts watch the game, took the name "Sabermetrics" from the group's initials: SABR.

Why do some players switch-hit?

Right-handed batters often hit better against left-handed pitchers, while lefty batters do well versus righty pitchers. So why not do both? By learning to switch-hit, batting either right- or left-handed, a batter can always have an advantage, no matter which hand the pitcher throws with!

WHY DON'T AMERICAN LEAGUE PITCHERS HAVE TO BAT?

In order to create higher scores in baseball, the American League took the bat out of the hands of poor-hitting pitchers beginning in 1973. Since then, each AL team can include one designated hitter, who does not play a position on the field. Today, just about every baseball league on the planet allows the DH, with the exception of the National League.

Why was there "no joy in Mudville?"

Because "Mighty Casey has struck out!" Spoiler alert: That's the ending of the most famous baseball poem of all time, *Casey at the Bat*. In the epic poem, the fictional town of Mudville's great sports hero had a chance to knock in the winning runs in the big game, but couldn't come through. The hometowns fans were, indeed, joyless. The poem was written by Ernest Thayer in 1888.

CASEY

Why do some race cars have wings?

The faster a car travels, the greater its *lift*, or tendency to rise off the roadway. When lift becomes too great, it causes the car to lose its grip on the road, making it hard to control. To prevent this, race cars often have wing-shaped parts called *spoilers* on the back. As air moves over the spoilers, a downward force is created that helps keep the car on the road.

Alert: spoilers!

WHY ARE NASCAR RACERS CALLED STOCK CARS?

The regular cars kept in stock by car dealers are called *stock* cars. In the early years of NASCAR, that's what racers drove. Over time, drivers began to use cars built especially for racing, but the name remains. NASCAR stands for National Association of Stock Car Auto Racing.

WHY DO RACE CARS HAVE ROLL CAGES?

On race cars, heavy metal frames—roll cages—extend above and around the driver. The cages are designed to protect the driver in a crash, even if the rest of the car falls apart around them.

roll bar

Réfrigération Gagné

Old-time stock cars were not as fast as today's models.

Why do some race cars run on smooth tires?

Regular tires have raised treads to channel water in wet conditions. That's not needed in NASCAR, where races don't run on wet tracks. The more rubber that meets the road, the more grip the race car has. So NASCAR and Formula 1 cars use tires with no tread at all. This allows the entire tire surface to touch the roadway. Formula 1 racers sometimes switch to wet-weather tires.

WHY ARE STOCK CARS SO COLORFUL?

It costs millions of dollars to run a NASCAR racing team. A lot of that money comes from sponsors who decorate the cars like rolling billboards. Companies pay big bucks to splash their colors, stickers, and logos on cars they sponsor. The more sponsors, the more colors a car might have!

WHY DO RACE CAR DRIVERS OFTEN DRIVE SO CLOSE TO EACH OTHER?

Race car drivers have perfected a racing technique called drafting. It is illegal to do this sort of tailgating on the highway, but it works well on the race track. Drafting takes advantage of an aerodynamic effect that lets a car use less energy to move as fast as the car in front of it. The lead car whizzes down the track, pushing the air out of the way. By racing inches away from the back of the lead car, the trailing car hits less air resistance, saving fuel and building up the momentum to pass at just the right moment. Don't try this at home!

Why do soccer players "bend" the ball?

By striking the outside of the ball as they kick it, talented soccer players can put tremendous spin on the ball. This spinning action makes the ball turn in the air like a baseball curveball (see page 173). They can bend the ball around a wall of players or into a corner of the goal. Kicking with the inside of the right foot bends the ball to the left; using the outside of the same foot creates a bend to the right.

(see page 173).

WHY IS SOCCER ALSO CALLED FOOTBALL AND *FUTBOL*?

Most of the world calls this sport football, but Americans call it soccer. That's to avoid confusion with the American version of football. The word soccer comes from an early name for the game, *association football*. Association became assoc.; assoc. became soccer. *Futbol* is the name of the game in Spanish-speaking countries.

WHY ARE RED CARDS BAD NEWS IN SOCCER?

Soccer referees show players red cards for making serious fouls, usually involving danger to another player. If a player is shown a red card, he or she is out of the game (and in some cases, the team's next game). That player can't be replaced, which leaves that team one player short. Two yellow cards, issued for lesser fouls, equal a red.

A red card means get out, and stay out.

Why do hockey goalies wear masks?

Facing a hard, rubber puck flying at more than 100 mph (91.4 kph), hockey goalies need all the padding they can get. The heavy-duty masks protect their faces and heads from getting hit by the puck or another player's stick. Amazingly, hockey was played for more than 80 years before goalies regularly wore masks. Not surprisingly, those goalies were known for having very few teeth.

Today's hockey masks protect players better.

Why do hockey players "check" each other?

Control of the puck is key to success in hockey. One way to get the puck away from an opponent—or get the opponent away from the puck—is to bang into them with your body, usually with your shoulder or chest. This legal play is called a *check*, and makes for some teeth-rattling action in this fast-paced game. Players who check to the head, use their stick when checking, or trip an opponent receive penalties. They have to learn to keep their checks in check!

Why do **golf balls** have dimples?

The first golfers found out quickly that scuffed-up golf balls fly farther than smooth ones. Over the years, golf ball makers experimented with all sorts of bumps, ridges, and divots to find the perfect pattern. The slight depressions, called dimples, have proven the most effective. The dimples give a golf ball lift by creating a layer of fast-moving air on the top of the ball and a layer of slower-moving air on the bottom of the ball. Depending on the brand, there might be 400 (or more) dimples on one ball.

WHY ARE METAL GOLF CLUBS CALLED WOODS?

Golfers use three basic types of clubs: woods, irons, and putters. For centuries, those first two words described the material used to make the clubheads. Irons are still made of metal, but about 30 years ago, club makers started using lightweight metals where they once used wood. Even though the material changed, the name of the type of club— a larger-headed tool used to hit the ball a long way—hasn't changed.

WHY ARE SHEEP PART OF GOLF'S HISTORY?

Without sheep, there are no shepherds. Without shepherds and their staffs, there might not be golf. According to most golf historians, the game developed in Scotland in the 1400s. Bored shepherds took to using their crooked-headed staffs to knock rocks around the pastures. Over time, they turned their pastime into an organized game, hitting small balls into tiny holes . . . all while the sheep watched patiently.

Why is the top prize in tennis called a Grand Slam?

In 1924, the International Lawn Tennis Federation decided that four international events—the U.S., French, and Australian Opens, and the All-England Championships at Wimbledon—were the major tennis events of the year. In 1933, the term Grand Slam was first used to describe the four annual tennis majors. In the card game of bridge, a grand slam means to win all of the hands. The first person to actually win the tennis Grand Slam—all four events in one year—was American Don Budge, in 1938.

WHY IS A ZERO CALLED LOVE IN TENNIS?

There are several theories, but no certain answer to this question. One of the most interesting, though, is that it is a mispronunciation of *l'ouef* (pronounced "loof"), which sounds sort of like love. L'ouef is the French word for egg, which looks sort of like a zero. However, French tennis players don't say their score is an egg. They say their score is . . . zero!

Why are tennis balls fuzzy?

Tennis balls are made of rubber. Without their fuzzy felt covering they would bounce too high and move too fast to play with. The fuzz on the outside creates drag in the air and friction when it hits the racket or playing surface.

181

Why is there a torch at the Olympic Games?

The flame that burns throughout the Games is a symbol created by the modern Games' founder, Pierre de Coubertin. For each Olympics, the flame is lit in Olympia, Greece, by the sun's rays. A relay then moves the flame from there to the host city. The first multi-country torch relay was held for the Berlin Games of 1936.

WHY WERE THERE NO OLYMPICS IN 1916, 1940, AND 1944?

The modern Olympics have been held every four years since they began in 1896, with three exceptions. In 1916, World War I was raging in Europe, so the games were cancelled. The 1940 Winter and Summer Olympics were scheduled to be held in Japan, but that nation had played a role in starting World War II, so those Games were cancelled, too. The 1944 Summer and Winter Games were set for London and Italy, but were not held, either, due to the ongoing war. The Games returned for good in 1948.

Why does the Olympic flag have five rings?

The rings were created in 1913 by Baron Pierre de Coubertin. He designed the five rings to represent five continents. (He was not including Australia and Antarctica!) The colors don't match up to any particular continents. De Coubertin chose them because he believed that every national flag at the time had at least one of the six colors, including the flag's white background.

Why are Olympic medals made of different metals?

The highest honor for any Olympic athlete is to win a gold medal. During the ancient Games, winners received olive wreaths to wear on their heads. The tradition of giving medals to the winners began at the Olympic Games in 1896. At that time, the winners who placed first did not get gold medals. Instead they received silver. Those who came in second took home a bronze medal, and third place finishers received nothing.

Why are Winter and Summer Olympics held in different years?

They used to be held in the same calendar year. The main reason for splitting them up—to be held once every two years—was to help get more attention for the Winter Games, which are not generally as popular as the Summer Games. The International Olympic Committee also wanted to try to increase the money paid by TV networks to air each of the Games. The last time both Games were held in the same year was 1992.

WHY DOES GREECE WALK FIRST IN THE OLYMPIC PARADE?

As the home of the original Olympics, Greece is given the honor of leading the nations of the world at all modern Olympics. The host nation always enters last, to the delight of hometown fans.

Why do water polo players wear special headgear?

Those caps might look a little silly, but they have two main purposes. First, since players are just wearing small bathing suits, the caps are their uniform. Each team wears a different color, while numbers on the hats identify the players for fans and officials. Second, the plastic on the side of the caps protects a player's ears from getting hit by the ball or by another player, either by accident . . . or on purpose!

Why do kitesurfers wear a harness?

Kitesurfers need to control a kite flying many feet above them. The power of the wind can give the kite more force than a person can handle just using two arms. So the kite is attached to a harness vest the riders wear. This lets them use the strength of their body along with their arms to control the kite as they skim over the water. Special latches on the vest let the rider release the kite in an emergency.

WHY DO SURFERS "HANG TEN"?

Mostly they do it to show how good they are at surfing. The term means to stand at the very front of the surfboard with all ten toes "hanging" off the edge. It's not an easy trick and can usually only be done on a heavy longboard when the back of the board is covered by the wave.

WHY CAN SNOWBOARDERS DO SUCH COOL TRICKS?

Physics and skill are the two things snowboarders need to perform amazing tricks. They need snow and a board, too! The boarders use the friction between the board and the snow to control their speed. By twisting their body to lean one way or another, they can turn, twist, and spin, using the edges of the board to create more friction as they dig into the snow. Riders build up speed that translates to momentum that keeps them in the air long enough to demonstrate their gymnastic ability, too!

Snowboarders can grab fat air thanks to science!

Why do skiers **wax their skis?**

Wax on the bottom of a snow ski or snowboard reduces the friction between the ski and the snow. Less friction turns into more speed as the skier flows down the slope.

Why do **bobsledders start outside their sleds?**

The faster a bobsled team pushes their bobsled at the start of their run, the more momentum the sled has. Momentum reduces the impact of air and friction on the moving sled, so it will go faster. Saving even one-tenth of a second during the start of a race can save one-third of a second on the entire bobsled run—which could be the difference between winning and losing.

Why do racehorses wear blinders

When running a race, a horse often wears a mask over its head. On the side of the mask are small plastic cups called blinders. These block a horse's peripheral vision—the ability to see things out of the corner of the eye. This lets the horse focus all of its attention on the track in front of it.

WHY DO HORSES WEAR SHOES?

Just as your shoes protect the bottoms of your feet, horseshoes protect a horse's feet. Humans nail or glue the shoes onto the hooves, which have no nerve endings, and are believed to feel no pain.

Horseshoes can protect against split hooves.

Why is horse racing's biggest prize called the Triple Crown?

Since 1877, horse racing fans have considered the top three Thoroughbred races in the country to be the Kentucky Derby, the Preakness, and the Belmont Stakes. *The New York Times* was the first to call the trio the "triple crown of American racing," in 1923. Seven years later, a horse named Gallant Fox was the first to win the honor now called the Triple Crown. Another horse, Sir Barton, had won all three races in 1919, but this feat was not yet known as the Triple Crown.

Why was the Iditarod inspired by heroes?

Since it began in 1973, the annual Iditarod sled dog race has sometimes topped 1,100 miles (1,770 km) across frozen Alaskan fields. The Iditarod trail itself is much older—it follows the path of a famous 1925 rescue mission. That year, dozens of sled-dog drivers created a relay that carried vital medicine from Seward to Nome, Alaska, in time to help sick people.

WHY DO AGILITY DOGS CRAWL THROUGH TUNNELS?

They're racing! In agility events, handlers direct dogs through an obstacle course. The dogs have to jump over barriers, run up and down ramps, crawl through tunnels, and more. It's a fast-moving sport for high-energy dogs who give it their all.

Why do robot jockeys ride camels?

In camel races in Saudi Arabia, robot jockeys replaced the small children who used to do the job. So many children were being hurt or mistreated that officials finally came up with a safer, saner solution. Since 2002, small robots have ridden atop the camels. They are remote controlled by drivers following in cars. A speaker in the robot's body lets the driver actually talk to the camel during the race, shouting commands or encouragement.

Why do people toss a caber?

A caber is a long, wooden pole that measures up to 20 feet (6.1 m) long and weighs as much as 200 pounds (90. 7 kg). As part of the Scottish Highland Games, and as a test of strength, people try to flip the heavy pole end over end. It requires power and balance to keep the pole from tipping over before you toss it!

WHY IS SEPAK TAKRAW SO DIFFICULT?

Imagine playing volleyball with a small ball . . . using only your feet! This game is popular in Asia. Players are able to leap high and smash the ball over the net like a volleyball spike. They use gymnastics moves to keep the ball in the air and earn points.

Why is the player in black holding her breath?

She is following the rules of kabaddi. In this sport, popular in Southeast Asia, one player has to raid enemy territory, tag an opponent, and return safely. The trick? They have to make their raid on only one breath. They chant the word *kabaddi* over and over to show judges they are not inhaling. The other team, of course, can grab them before they get back. It's a breathtaking, action-packed game of fast moves.

Why do **people race in a bog?**

In a squishy, wet, gooey, leech-infested bog in Wales, contestants in the annual Bog Snorkeling World Championships plunge in to take their fastest lap. Anything to win a championship, right? There is also a mountain-biking version of this down-and-dirty race.

Water buffalo make sport of the mud just like humans. In several Asian countries, drivers steer water buffalo through mud-covered tracks to see who has the fastest team.

Why do people run mud races?

Chances are, they think it's fun! Mud, water, and fire-strewn obstacle course racing has become a popular fitness activity. Groups of people often race together. They compete to see who is the fastest . . . and, of course, who gets the messiest!

189

c: center; t: top; b: bottom; r: right; l: left.

BK: BigStock, DT: Dreamstime, DP: Dollar Photo, IS: IStock, SS: Shutterstock, PL: PhotoLibrary.

BACK COVER
Kelly Richardson/IS t; Warangkana Charuyodhim/DT b.

ANIMALS
4: Lukas Mislek/DT. 6: Kelly Richardson/IS t; Aleksandar Mijatovic/DP bl; belizar/DP 6bc. 7: Steffen Foerster/DT t; Donald Gargano/SS b. 8: Shutterstock/SS t; adrianciurea69/DP b. 9: Matt Jeppson/DP t; Jason Aspinall/DT c; Bierchen/DT b; Sikth/DT inset. 10: Casanowe/DP c; Aussieanouk/DP b. 11: Cathy Keifer/DT t; NOAA b. 12: Juniors Bildarchiv t; Sergey Taran/DT b 13: Ivan Tihelka/DT t; Jorg Drews/IS b. 14: Anekoho/DT t; Meisterphotos/DT c; michaklootwijk/DP b. 15: Markmirror/SS t; Pearson Art Photo/SS b. 16: mbridger68/DP t; Paul Banton/DT c; Aquanaut4/DT br; Cbpix/SS bl. 17: Yuval Helfman/DP t; Brad Whitsitt/SS b. 18: DnDavis/DT t; Hel080808/DT b 19: Andreanita/DP t; Salajean/DP c; Taviphoto/DT b. 20: Yann Hubert/DT t; Michael Robbins/DP br; Nicram Sabod/SS bl. 21: Brendan Howard/SS l; M.P. Imageart/SS r 22: JustASC/SS t; rck/DP br; Andrea Izzotti/DP bl 23: Sutisa Kangvansap/DT t; Palex66/DT b.

EARTH
24: Mayra Pau/DT. 26: Ratpack 2/DT t; Oxford Scientific (OSF)/PL b. 27: Victor Zastolskiy/BK. 28: MISR Team/NASA t; Fogstock LLC/PL b. 29: Juliengrondin/SS l; Bychkov Kirill Alexandrovich/SS r. 30: Ibird/SS t; Lunamarina/DT b31: Francisco Caravana/DT t; Rovenko Design/SS b. 32: Monika Wisniewsak/DT t; Igomezc/Wikimedia b. 33: NASA r; MSIR Team/NASA l. 34: Lee Prince/SS l; Christina Richards/SS b; Wusuowei/DP tr. 35: Nucleogomos/DT tr; Kokoroyuki/DT tl; Sandpiper/DP bl. 36: Epic Stock/SS t; Michael Gil/Wiki bl. 37: Anemone Projectors/Wiki t; Europics/Newscom. 38: Vasily Smirnov/DT t; Jan Martin Will/SS b. 39: Katherine Martin/DP bkgd; Anastasia Pyryeva/DP tr; Slimsepp/DP tc; Jeff Hammond/DT c; Zentilia/SS b.

SPACE
40: NASA. 42: NASA (2). 43: NASA t; Lee Gillion/DT br; NASA/Bill Ingalls b. 44: NASA t, bl; Mary Evan Pic. Lib/PL br. 45: NASA/Goddard Flight Center t; NASA/JPL b. 46: NASA/Jaxa t; JPL/Caltech/NASA b. 47: JPL/Caltech/NASA. 48: NASA/Johns Hopkins University Applied Physics Laboratory/Southwest Research Institute t, b, 49: NASA (2). 50: JPL-Caltech/NASA t; Marshall Space Flight Center/NASA b. 51: NASA t; Andyvic/DT b. 52: NASA t; NASA/JPL b. 53: Library of Congress Prints and Photographs Division t; Sven Herman/IS b.

HUMANS
54: Soonwh/DP. 56: Razyph/DT. 57: Tracy Whiteside/DT t; Uklas/DP b. 58: Mark Shulman t; Kantver/DT b. 59: Ulzana/DT t; Blantiag/DP b. 60: Quan Yin/SS t; Jane Brennecker/BK t. 61: Stefan Hermans/DT bl; Xavier Gallego Morell bc; Katalinks/DT br. 62: Luis Santos/SS t; Warangkana Charuyodhim/DT b. 63: Korhan Hasim Isik/IS t; Khrozhevska/DT b. 64: EdBockStock/SS b; Nerify/DT t. 65: USDA (chart); Margot555/DT tl; Kenishirotie/DT bl; Juri Samsonov/DT cr; Anandkrish/DT tr; Christian Jung/DT br. 66: Valentyn Volkov/SS t; Gbh007/DT b. 67: Geir-Olav Lyngfjell b; Kazoka303030/DP t; Dml5050 r. 68: Umberto Leporini/DT t; Leungchopan/DT b. 69: Jeka/SS t; Artofphoto/SS b. 70: TheBlackRhino/DT t; Denisnata/DT b. 71: Godfer/DT t; Jorg Hackemann/DT b. 72: Atholpady/DT b; Dvmsimages/DT t. 73: Elenathewise/DT t; Esben Hansen/DT b. 74: Ntdanai/DT t; Ljupco/DT b. 75: Ivonne Wierink/DT t; Dolgachov/DT b. 76: Jamen Percy/DT t; Kvitka Fabian/SS b; Igor Stepovik/IS r. 77: Orangeline/DT t; Rob/DP b.

AROUND THE WORLD
78: Vladimirkz/DT 78. 80: Derrick Neill/DT t; Howard Sandler/DT bl; Luciano Mortula/SS br. 81: Ershamstar/DT t; Tinnaporn Sathapornnanont/DT b. 82 Steve Estvanik/SS t; Bryan Busovicki/SS b. 83: Egot450/DT t; Hugarian Tourism Board c; Sfmthd/DT b. 84: Attila Jandi/DT t; Jeremy Richards/DT b. 85: Scott Rothstein/SS t; Maksym Gorpenyuk/SS b. 86: Jesse Kraft/DT t; Eg004713/DT b. 87: Edurivero/DT t. 88: Aliaksandr Mazurkevich/DT t; Jorg Hackemann/DT cl; Sophie Mcaulay/DT b. 89: Sean Pavone Photo/DP t; Platongkoh/DT b. 90: Imagesource/PL b; Pavel Dudek/SS t. 91: Xvaldes/DT t; Photolook/Fotolia b. 92: Alexey Belov/DT t; Pavel Losevsky/DT t. 93: Imagicity/Wikimedia t; Dewaal Venter/DT c; Patricia Hofmeester/DT b.

HISTORY
94: Umb-o/DP. 96: Enrico Beccari/BK l; Janne Ahvo/IS r. 97: Andesign/SS t;. Quintanilla/SS r. 98: Dmitry Rukhlenko/SS. 99: Darren Baker/DT t; Ronnie Chua/DT c; Photographerlondon/DT b. 100: Willem85/DT t; Kaspars Grinvalds/DT c; Jurand/SS b. 101: J. Robert Fleury/Wiki t; Miklav/Fotolia b. 102: Istvan Csak/DT t; Copiste inconnu/Wiki c; John Pine/Bonhams/Wiki b. 103: T-stock/SS r; North Wind Archives/PL l; Songsak Paname/DT b. 104: North Wind Archives/PL. 105: Songquan Den/DT t; Painting by Michael A. Hayes b. 106: Brownscombe/Wiki t; Jenny Thompson/DP b. 107: Hulton Archive/IS t. 108: LunaMarina/DT t; Caitlin Mirra/SS b. 109: National Archive/Navy History and Heritage Command t; Library of Congress br; Gary Blakeley/DT bl. 110: Big Stock t; Library of Congress b. 111: Big Stock. 113: Library of Congress t; Mary Evans Picture Library/PL b. 114: US Army b; Library of Congress c. 115: Everett Historical/SS t; Soren Pilman/IS b. 116: Angel Dibilio/SS t; Bundesarchiv b. 117: National Archives and Records Administration; Anusom62/DT b. 118: Enrico Beccari/BK t; Cardaf/SS b. 119: Library of Congress t; Oomf Inc. c; David Shankbone/Wiki r. 120: Dimaberkut/DT t; Time Inc. c; US Supreme Court b. 121: Pixelrobot/DT t; Office of the President tr; EPA bl; Brandon Tucker/DT br. 122: NASA t, l; NARA c. 123: US Army inset; US Air Force t; Gail Benson/DT. 124: Office of the President t (2); Debra Saucedo/DT b. 125: Yoshiyuki Kaneko/DT t; Massimo Tiga Pellicciardi/Flickr c; Neneo/DT b.

SCIENCE
126: Beerfan/DP. 128: Svand/SS t; Alexander Raths/DT b. 129: Iakov Filminov/DT t; Airborne77 b. 130: Kitch Bain/SS t; Jordache/DT b. 131: Ilona75/DT b. 132: Warren Rosenberg/BK l; Pavel Shchegolev/SS r. 133: Vkovalcik/DT t; Fred/Fotolia b. 134: Tyler Olson/DT; Iourii Tcheka/SS r. 135: Valentyn Volkov/SS t; Jules315 b (2). 136: Steve Cukrov/SS t; Nataliya PeregudovabSS. 137: Thawats/DT t; Mgkuijkpers/DT b. 138: Adventure Stock/SS t; Brykaylo Yuriy b; Kichigin/DT flake; Ankevanwyk/DT cup. 139: Iphotos/SS t; George Kroll/DT inset t; Santos06/DT inset b; Ovidiu Iordache/DT b. 140: Ooyoo/IS t; Jagcz/DT b. 141: Vera Kuttelvaserova/DP t; Eddydegroot/DT c; Webitect/DT b. 142: Gelpi/SS t; Adaychou/DT c inset; Studio Foxy/SS b inset; Melinda Fawver/SS b. 143: Ragnarok/SS 143; Hanschr/DT c; Gmf1000i/DT b. 144: Perkus/SS t; Kieran Mithani/IS b. 145: Giulianocoman/DT tr; Lily/DP tl; Elnur/DT b.

TECH
146: Rawpixelimages/DT. 148: Romantiche/DT t; Monkey Business Images/DT b. 149: Leungchopan/DT t; Reshoot/DT b. 150: Gchutka/IS. 151: Alphaspirit/DT tr; Mrhighsky/DT c; Johan Larson/DP b. 152: Tsian/SS t; 3dmentat/DP b. 153: Nitroxelmares/DT tr; Gchutka/IS b. 154: Babar760/DT tl; Stefan1179/DP c. 155: Library of Congress t; Aaron Amat/SS b. 156: Perkus/SS t; Iancucristi/DT inset; Lisa F. Young/SS b. 157: Epicstock/DT tr; William87/DP. 158: McKown/DT t; Jhernan124/DT c; Brackishnewzealand/DT b. 159: Library of Congress t; Absente b. 160: Lutherhill/IS l; Martin D. Vonka/SS tr; Marianvejcik/DT b. 161: Photographerlondon/DT t; Rocketclips/DT c; Courtesy Organovo b.

SPORTS
162: Paparazzofamily/DT. 164: Eugene Buchko/SS t; Dazhetalk/DT c; Phil McDonald/DT b. 165: Yobroso/DT t; Pongphan Ruengchai/DT c; Brandon Tucker/DT b. 166: Rico Leffanta/DT t; Elisanth/DT b. 167: Briancweed/DT t; Felix Mizioznikov/SS b. 168: Wavebreakmedia/DT t; Patty Kelley b. 169: Pete Saloutos/SS t; Nicholas Piccillo/DT c; Catwalker/DT b. 170: Michael Flippo/DT r; Scott Prokop/DT l. 171: Eq Roy/DT t; SPG l; Kelpfish/DT bkgd. 172: Americanspirit/DT t; Aldo Di Bari Murga/DT b. 173: Amy Myers/DT bl; Aspenphoto/DT br. 174: Tressiedavis/DT; Anton Donev/DT b. 175: Cynthia Farmer/DT t; Ron and Joe/SS b. 176: Supertramp/DT t; Raytags/DT bl; Peter Weber/SS br. 177: Doug James/SS. 178: Fotokostic/SS t; Rui Alexandre Araujo/SS b. 179: Websubstance/DT t; iofoto/DT b. 180: Godfer/DT tl; D2xed/DT cl; Pictac/DT cr; Twvogleast/DT br. 181: Trentham/DT t; Maxisport/DP bl; Cobalt88/DT br. 182: Rerveridis/DT tl; Lazyllama/DT tr. 183: Seregal/DT tl; Neasu Razram Chirnoaga/DT cl; MaxiSports/DT cr; Dennis Kornilov/SS b. 184: NicoSmit/DT t; Withgod/DT b. 185: Ilja Masik/SS t; Jonathan Larsen b. 186: Jacqueline Abromeit/SS l; Cynoclub/SS r. 187: Kirk Geisler/DT t; Natalie Heath/DT c; Sean Nel/SS b. 188: Rico Leffanta/DT t; Manit Larpluechai/DT c; Pariyawit Sukumpantanasarn/DT b. 189: Wikipedia t; Nopparatk/DT c; Quenofrock/DT b.